THE CREATIVE WEDDING HANDBOOK

THE
CREATIVE WEDDING HANDBOOK

Wendy Somerville Wall

NEWMAN PRESS
New York • Paramus, N. J. • Toronto

Illustrations by Bette S. Baker
Book designed by William H. Baker

Copyright © 1973 by Wendy Somerville Wall

Library of Congress
Catalog Card Number: 72-93983

ISBN 0-8091-0177-7

Published by Newman Press
Editorial Office: 1865 Broadway
N.Y., N.Y. 10023

Business Office 400 Sette Drive,
Paramus, N.J. 07652

Printed and bound in the
United States of America

For John
With whom every day is celebration
(mostly)

CONTENTS

ACKNOWLEDGMENTS

This book was born on a wedding day when my brother and his wife, Grant and Gigi, made all of us feel a very, very special part of their happiness. To them, thank you. It grew and developed as other couples generously shared their day. To Michele and Myron, Ann and Charles, Joanne and Larry, Christine and Tom, Anne and Brian, Maureen and Tom, Barbara and Dick, Susan and David, Maureen and Denis, Nancy and Bill, Kathy and Mark, Kathy and Tom, Karen and Ed, Mina and Bruce, Grace and Sam, Margaret and Patrick, Jan and Dean, Nancy and John, Simone and John, Katherine and Kenneth, thank you.

To all the celebrants who presided at these wedding feasts, thank you. But I am especially indebted to Joe Lavoie, Kevin Kelly, Patrick Morris O.F.M., and the communities at Emmaus House and U Conn who first showed me warm and loving and jubilant liturgy.

Ken Meltz of the Paulist Information Center in Boston provided invaluable thoughts on music preparation and the musicianship of Eddie Bonnemere of the Community of St. Thomas the Apostle in Harlem and Gil Robbins of St. Joseph's, New York City, has vividly demonstrated for me the role of an inspiring music director. I heard the voices of Jeanne Lewin and the folk group at Immaculate Conception parish, Westhampton Beach, New York sing many of these songs and prove that they are right.

For the conversation of Rev. Gerald Sigler and Paul Jones, S.J., of the Woodstock Center for Religion and Worship, I am grateful. And of Donna Ford in the N.C. News library at the United States Catholic Conference, I am most appreciative.

The excellent commentary of Rev. Robert W. Hovda in "The Rite for Celebrating Marriage During Mass," in the *Manual of Celebration,* published by The Liturgical Conference, Washington, D.C., inspired many of these couples and thus inspired me. Harvey Cox's *Feast of Fools* delightfully stirred up my thinking.

To my editor, Don Brophy, and his wife, Pat, who listened at odd hours, to my husband John who unfailingly believed a deadline more important than dinner, to Jonathan, age two, who enthusiastically believed a book could be written with him on my lap, and to Clinton who waited to be born until the book was finished, "I love you five."

He who knows love brings
God and the world together.
—*Martin Buber*

WHY THIS BOOK AND HOW TO USE IT

To be honest, it must be admitted that the first part of this chapter is really a foreword, a personal indulgence of the author. It isn't called that because people often skip forewords. The second part of the chapter is a "backword." Please read it (and while you're at it, read the first part, too).

The Sacrament As Witness

It has been our privilege lately to come away from a wedding liturgy with a sense of renewal, of sacrament, of grace touching the couple married and touching ourselves and the community with whom we shared the wedding.

Why? Because of its nature a wedding is like that. It is a joyful sacrament created by God to bestow his grace. Few go to any wedding without some small recognition that God is there. On its own, without any help from its friends, the sacrament is witness to the love of God whose gift it is. The marriage sacrament is more. The covenant between man and woman symbolizes the covenant between God and his people. Marriage is a lovely sacrament indeed.

Yet, why did I miss some of this? Why was I coming from wedding after wedding touched momentarily (at least consciously) by the mystery, but more caught up in how the bride looked, the flowers, the grandeur of the organ, the skipping of the flower girl? Probably because I am one of those people who daydream, who stand in the rear behind rows of flowered hats and drift off from the tableau forward. I am one of those people who need to be told, who have to be. . . led.

1

And lately our friends have been joyously, deliberately, leading me, all of us, to come away from their ceremony, missing little, exclaiming, "I really felt a part of that wedding." I have witnessed the marriage of a couple and affirmed that God is good. I have whispered to my husband during the moment of their consent, my own "yes!" I have understood better the significance of the sacrament in its wider context; as Erich Fromm says, "Love for one person implies love for man as such." I have absorbed the clothes the bride wore, the flowers, the music, the festivity and thought them one with the mystery.

What has made me so profoundly grateful for weddings? At root, Rome, the spirit of Vatican II and the documents which came from it, for these have been the source of a couple's freedom to participate more fully in the expression of their marriage. At root, too, today's more relaxed etiquette, for weddings have always had their parallel religious and social ritual.

The Constitution on the Sacred Liturgy as promulgated by Paul VI in 1962 is a most exciting invitation to the People of God to use all of their resources, all of their talents in testimony of their faith. The constitution describes the liturgy as "... the most outstanding means whereby the faithful may express in their lives and manifest to others, the mystery of Christ and the real nature of the Church." Of the sacraments in particular the constitution proclaims their purpose " ... to sanctify men, to build up the body of Christ and finally to give worship to God; because they are signs they also instruct."

How serious, but happy, a responsibility is placed on the marrying couple. Not only must they prepare their own souls for the reception of the sacrament, they are challenged by their faithful act of celebrating to stimulate the attitude of their guests toward a more open reception of grace, a more thoughtful worship of God, and a more active love of neighbor.

The new Rite of Marriage promulgated in the United States in 1970 provides a medium within which a couple can work out their personal message to the community. There are eight choices among Old Testament readings, ten among New Testament readings, ten among the Gospels, and numerous

2

choices of psalms and alleluias. There are decisions to be made by the bride and groom among several optional prayers, blessings, and prefaces. The marriage consent exchanged by the couple need no longer come after the prodding of the priest in an awkward "repeat-after-me" moment, but now is encouraged to be memorized or read, often in words composed by the couple. There is built into the rite the opportunity for considerable freedom in movement and gesture, in the method of entering and exiting, in the position at the altar, in the use of witnesses, in the presentation of the offertory gifts, in the kiss of peace. Music and song selections can reflect the participatory climate.

Among all the Church's liturgical rituals, the marriage ritual has historically been the most open to local interpretations. It is intriguing to see the Constitution on the Sacred Liturgy praise a statement from the Council of Trent, 1563: "If any regions are wont to use other praiseworthy customs and ceremonies when celebrating the sacrament, the sacred Synod earnestly desires that these be wholly retained."

The introduction to Rome's officially promulgated Rite of Marriage continues the latitude given local custom: "The formulas of the Roman Ritual may be adapted or, as the case may be, filled out... When the Roman Ritual has several optional formulas, local rituals may add other formulas of the same type... Within the rite of the sacrament of matrimony, the arrangement of its parts may be varied... As for marriage customs of nations that are now receiving the gospel for the first time, whatever is good and not indissolubly bound up with superstition and error should be sympathetically considered and, if possible, preserved intact... Each conference of bishops may draw up its own marriage rite suited to the usages of the place and people and approved by the Apostolic See...."

Nevertheless, the United States Conference of Bishops issued a marriage rite very little distinct from that of Rome: it adds an additional choice of formula for marriage vow and final blessing. But the conference has given discretion to local bishops, advised, hopefully, by their diocesan liturgical commissions, to modify the ritual. Official flexibility, as shown by chancery guidelines, is, however, pretty taut. Officially, too, the guidelines are enforced in varying degrees.

3

Bishops differ in their pastoral outlook. Within reason much is left to the local pastor. Pastors differ, too.

The weddings which so inspired us were not all within the strict interpretation of the rubric. They were, however, cheerfully within the spirit of the original freedom-permitted custom to adapt, to fill out, and to vary. Perhaps in the minds of the priests who celebrated these weddings the creativity, sensitivity, and community orientation of the "youth culture" (even though not all of these couples were young in years) qualified them as a distinct "region" or "nation." The Woodstock nation maybe. More often, simply people, couples in more or less traditional clothes, surrounded by approving guests, who value the integrity of the ritual as shape and form and familiarity, but must also work out their own expression within the plan. Couples who understand a wedding ritual as uniting them uniquely in a role past, present, and future, but, above all, present.

The wedding rituals I share with you are not "from the underground." Some were celebrated on campus and some in experimental worshiping communities. True that the closer you come to places where liturgy and theology are studied, the more dimension the couple is allowed in developing their ceremony. Yet most of these weddings were celebrated in parish churches by parish priests.

What all share, in addition to a bride and groom who cared very much about the witness of their wedding, is a celebrant who cared and spent time in helping the couple choose readings and gestures and write vows and prayers that expressed what they brought to marriage and sought from it.

As one priest observed, "Working with a couple as they design their liturgy has enormous pastoral possibilities for me. It can really be a time of counseling, a chance for us all to reflect on marriage, its personal and religious and social significance. When they choose among the options of the new rite I ask 'why this one and not that one?' When they want to say something that is not among the options, we discuss what there is about it that makes it so necessary to their wedding. The same with the music, how they use the space, everything. An examination of what they want to say and do tells me and, more importantly, them a great deal about the present and the future of their life together."

4

On the other hand, too many priests relate that they are eager to involve couples in their ceremony, but can't get them even to select among the options permitted. "You decide, Father. We just want to get married."

Which is nice. But how much more meaningful for us, the community, if we come away from your wedding knowing why *this* wedding. Some things don't need to be spoken, but it is better if they are.

How To Use This Book

There is danger in a book like this. In the following pages you can examine the ways in which many brides and grooms created their wedding day: how to handle a wedding. It would be possible, borrowing an ingredient here and one there, to work out a recipe for your own different and with-it ceremony. It would be possible and it might work if the other couple's "why" is truly your own. It could be very busy and artificial gimmickry, losing half your guests, destroying the community you seek. Ritual is fragile. There must be *your* balance, *your* integrity. The cake falls when the leaven is missing.

How to handle a wedding is to love it.

And how to read this book is critically, with a pencil. This is a workbook, meant to spark your imagination, not replace it. Mark it up, cross things out, scribble in the margins.

The marriage rite in the following chapters is presented in its official entirety within the context of the Mass most often celebrated in local parish churches. Some of you will want to or will be required to celebrate your wedding in this fashion.

Others of you will decide right away that this is altogether too much: too long, too wordy, too stilted. So you'll begin to edit, striking out a section of the Mass or a part of the rite, asking yourselves questions like, "Do we really need both a greeting from the Mass and an opening prayer from the rite?" and, when you merge them, deciding that the wording of neither really says it the way you want it said. So you write your own.

I hope that you'll so dislike an idea that it will determine or reinforce for you exactly what it is that you *do* want to do. "Sit down during our vows! We want everyone to leave their seats and come and stand in a circle around us."

I hope you'll say "yes" to a few things and find parts where you like the idea, but not precisely how it is expressed, so you change it.

The penitential rite in this book, for example, is presented as the original author wrote it. When I first discovered it in the wedding of a New York couple, however, it had been considerably altered. They had adapted it from a friend's ceremony, whose priest had borrowed it from another priest's wedding file, who had found it "somewhere," etc. Liturgy is not static. It is alive and well and living in all of us.

You might want to make the language of your ritual warmer, more personal, more conversational. When "we have come to celebrate..." becomes "we have come together today to celebrate..." it becomes somehow more human.

Don't be afraid to paraphrase, to substitute a word more comfortable to say for one that has no rhythm, to cut out an offending phrase. One bride, liking the Rebekkah story in the Old Testament, didn't like the part about Isaac's marriage consoling him for the death of his mother, so she struck that sentence, incidental to the story and not altering the context at all.

Contemplate the ritual. Many couples have found that rearranging the parts of the Mass and the elements of the rite have made the ceremony more meaningful to them. They have put the kiss of peace right after their exchange of vows so that immediately after they have become husband and wife they could move among their friends receiving their best wishes. They have joined their vows to the consecration so that the idea that the love and union and commitment of bride and groom is a sign of the love and union and commitment of Christ and his Church is more graphically illustrated. They have thought there is an awful lot of talking in this ceremony and have blended the nuptial and final blessings into one. They have, as the couple mentioned earlier did, moved the penitential rite to become part of the Prayer of the Faithful just before the offertory. Yet, if their ceremony has really worked, they have maintained a dignified and graceful language, however contemporary, and a

6

respect for the sculpture of ritual.

At some time during your ceremony you may want to read or have read a non-Scripture poem or passage or personally composed statement that has special significance to you. The temptation is to eliminate either an Old Testament (especially) or New Testament reading and substitute your selection for it. This makes sense because you don't want your ceremony to go on interminably while you try to say everything you have to say about your idea of marriage.

Still, I hope very much that you won't make this decision before you read through and think about the Scripture options of the official rite. Several in every category should delight you with their universality, their simplicity, their style and insight. In fact, couples have discovered that there is even a passage included among the options so much like a non-Scripture reading they had intended to use that the latter might almost be paraphrase.

Open-mindedly read the options, explore the Bible before you decide to interrupt the integrity of the Liturgy of the Word. "The answer, my friend, is blowin' in the wind." What did Dylan mean by wind? I don't know, but wind has long been a symbol for the Spirit who inspired the word, and that Spirit has a unique power to speak to our hearts.

If you decide not to place your secular reading in the Liturgy of the Word, or are prohibited from doing so, there are plenty of other opportunities for it: as a mood setter before the Mass begins, during the entrance rite, after your vows, at the offertory, the thanksgiving, the final blessing.

The Scripture readings in this book, incidentally, are taken from the *New English Bible* because the author enjoys the way they sound. You might find another Bible translation more appealing to you. At any rate, you will probably discover that the lectionary in your church uses a different translation. If you prefer, you might bring this book on the altar with you.

Marrying yourselves is really very simple. When you come right down to it, all that is absolutely necessary for a marriage to take place that is valid and licit in the eyes of the Church is that the priest ask for and receive your consent and bless that promise. All the rest illuminates your purpose.

Illuminate! Happy wedding!

PREPARING THE CELEBRATION

Setting the Date

"Congratulations! Best wishes! When?"

For some reason the first question people ask when you've made known your intention to get married is "when?" Family and friends are eager and anxious to pin you down to a point in time. It gives your promise to each other a feeling of solidarity, of permanence. Suddenly it's not that vague "someday" that everyone has been suspecting. You have made known your agreement, and the first pressure of your constituents is being applied. You have indeed "gone public."

"When?"

The date you pick is largely a matter of convenience — yours and that of the people you want to surround you on your wedding day. Occasionally "when" has to be determined by job commitments, school, or other rather limiting outside influences. Usually "when" can be when it is easiest and nicest for you. "When" should be when you can give your wedding some time and thought, a pleasant amount of anticipation to savor its meaning and plan its celebration, but

8

Real celebration links us
to a world of memories,
gestures, values and hopes
that we share with
a much larger community.
                    —*Harvey Cox*

not so much time that you lose your perspective in details.

"When" should have a certain soul-pleasing ambience about it. You like the smell and touch of this month of the year, you understand the sound of this day of the week, you glow in the look of this time of day.

Yet "when" has to be flexible. Arbitrarily setting a date and then finding out that other things don't fit with it can be devastating. Sometimes we let the date loom as a kind of symbol and anything which threatens that seems to threaten the whole thing.

Perhaps it is best to think of "on or about" until you determine what is most essential: the date itself or the time of day or the availability of a particular church or your choice of a reception place or the accommodation of your guests. When you've set your priorities everything else falls into place, because you are satisfied that the thing that is most important to you is going to be. Usually there is nothing about your wedding plans that can't be replaced by something almost as perfect when you relax and accept it.

"When" is the easy decision to make. Deciding what kind of wedding you will have and where you will have it is the super challenge to your understanding of marriage as a sacrament, a sign of love and unity. You want your wedding to bring people together and it will. It can be your gift to one another and to those who share the day with you. This as a goal will help you determine the externals of your ceremony.

Begin with where you're "at." What kind of a wedding do the two of you want? Certainly one that has the most meaning for you, one which honestly reflects the people you are, the things you enjoy, the goals and expectations you share for the future.

Meditate a bit on "a wedding." It is a moment in your time which, through its ritual, entwines you with the whole history of weddings and with the wedding at Cana. It's not everyday you're part of an epic; set it apart, make the most of it! You will want to preserve the ritual structure and at least as much of the tradition as communicates this. But you may choose, as many contemporary couples do, to highlight the Cana tradition, for Christ came to bless not a solemn and dignified ceremony, but a joyous feast.

Unless you have decided to marry before a small group of very like-thinking friends, you will come to realize that your wedding is not *your* wedding, not completely. Typically wedding guests share one thing: they have all come in a spirit of love to wish you well. Typically, too, they share little else.

You don't want any of the guests to be there only as audience, confused and uncomfortable onlookers. You want all to be, as far as possible, one in spirit, participants, comprehending and sharing the joy. "A festival," says Harvey Cox, "seems successful only when everyone has imbibed its spirit. If someone is left out, everyone feels the worse for it. Thus, the very essence of celebration is participation and equality, the abolition of domination and paternalism."

Planning Together

Planning a wedding together is an excellent test and advertisement of your maturity and readiness for marriage and, if you're listening, will give both of you insight into the nitty-gritty of the relationship you have with one another and with other people. In fact your reactions to the give-and-take of wedding planning are a preview of the after-wedding situation. For instance, does the man think most of the preparation is "woman's work" and not for his involvement, or does the woman exclude him from the arrangements? Don't be surprised if future host-and-hostessing and other things become one-way responsibilities.

If a decision is forced because of tears or tirade, then consistent behavior can be expected later.

You'll be told that the inevitable fatigue of prenuptial hassling is a legitimate excuse for temperament and to be expected of the bride and groom. I've since discovered that, once married, the same excuse is useful for Thanksgiving, Christmas, entertaining the boss, etc. It tends to dull a little of the joy of them all.

You can (try and) learn during your wedding preparation that hassle shared is high comedy, and fatigue catered to promptly and firmly seldom becomes overwhelming.

Once you, as a couple, have decided what is important to you in your wedding ceremony, you will bring your ideas to your parents.

Sometime during her stay in the hospital after you were born your mother looked at your father and said "someday she (he) will be getting married" and then they both had a vision of how it would be on that day. While you were growing up they imagined that picture periodically and it delighted and reassured them. Someday you would fit into their reference: falling in love, as they did; marrying, as they did; struggling to learn to live with one another, as they did; having children, as they did.

Maybe your ideas on weddings are one with your parents. Probably they differ somewhat or even a great deal. Don't sell parents short, however, before you've given them a chance. Your family is not as surprised or distressed as they might at first act by your decision to lift your wedding out of the well-worn rut. After all, they have lived with you all your life and surely you are not suddenly doing something completely out of character. And if you are, think again. To be different for its own sake is phony.

One bride's parents were not happy with the unorthodox invitations, the soft-rock music, the liturgy. Talking it over, the bride discovered what really hurt her mother was her plan to carry red roses, in her mother's mind a symbol of virginity lost! As it turned out the bride carried a traditional white bouquet, the mother planned the hors d'oeuvres, Dad

11

admitted he was flattered to be asked to read, and all were pleased by the warmth and good will of the lively wedding.

Some family disagreements are less easily solved than that, but start with the obvious approach to sharing: simply discussing your plans.

Choosing the Place

Perhaps the most "community" wedding you could have is one taking place in the parish church of both the bride and groom and their parents when the couple plan to live nearby. In our transient society this is happening less frequently. Many of today's couples have lived away from home for several years. They have built up a group of friends and probably worship with many of them, perhaps in a city church which is not their geographical parish. Still, they may decide to honor tradition and celebrate their marriage in the parish church of the bride's family.

The pastor of the bride's current territorial parish has jurisdiction over the wedding. It is to him you must go for a letter of permission if you plan to have your wedding elsewhere. Usually such permission is not difficult to get. However, if your objection to having the ceremony in the local church is that you want to have a less restricted ceremony than that particular church permits, it might be better, if you must give reasons, to stress other legitimate justifications in your approach to the pastor. Rarely a pastor sees this as his opportunity to indoctrinate you in his idea of good wedding form and refuses his permission.

The church and chapels of the diocesan cathedral are generally open to any couple in the diocese; one of these might better satisfy your wedding plans. For example, you may wish to be married in the late afternoon or evening, but this interferes with a local church's confession schedule; or you may wish a candlelight ceremony, and not every church has fire laws that can accommodate this.

Ideally you will be able to give the choice of a church uninhibited consideration and celebrate in one that both has meaning for you and lends itself most to the type of feeling you wish your wedding to have. There is a church that welcomes the music you choose, approves your desire to write your own vows, and can offer you the liturgical space

12

that creates the environment you want. If those things are truly important to you don't be lazy or shy about seeking them. Shop around.

Many churches are architecturally constructed to facilitate the increased participation of the laity in the liturgy. Our favorite wedding (my brother's), whose generous spirit and wisdom permeate this book, took full sensual advantage of the unique and inviting design of the Chapel of the Immaculate Heart of Mary, where the desert yields to foothills, outside Santa Fe, New Mexico. The liturgical space is simple and small and bright and open with seating so everyone can see. The nearness to the Santa Fe Center for Pastoral Liturgy and an innovative priest encourage flexibility in ritual content but respect the ritual and discourage bad art. Every bridal whim can't be satisfied.

Behind a window in the wall in back of where people are seated is a projection room. Slides can be effectively flashed on the wall directly behind or to the side of the altar. A song text, for example, projected on the wall encourages everyone to look up and out and sing and eliminates the distraction of books and mimeographed sheets. In this wedding the couple illustrated the text " . . . for this reason a man shall leave father and mother and cling to his wife . . . " with pictures of the bride as a baby with her family, the groom as a baby with his and one of themselves. It showed us all a little of what the "rite of passage" is about.

If you'd like such a church and can't find one, improvise. One couple startled, but happily did not dismay, their pastor when they requested permission to have their ceremony in the school gymnasium, usually a "church" only for the Sunday overflow. The Norman Gothic dignity of the main building they felt discouraged intimacy. In the gym they arranged folding chairs so that their friends encircled them during the ceremony.

Consider the features of the church in designing your visual wedding scheme. Perhaps modern stained-glass windows of yellow and lime green can influence your invitation, program, clothes, and banners or a stark, high-ceilinged church with a great aluminum Christ figure behind the altar might call for tall, slim, black and white and silver banners or ceiling drops.

Sometimes, however, you will find that the parish in which it is best for you to get married because of family and other considerations is not one which permits your "style" wedding: maybe no guitars, only traditional processionals, no secular readings, the text of the ritual left strictly alone. Fortunately the simplicity and significance of the revised rite need only your joyful attitude to embellish it. And no church so inhibits you that you can't, if you're ingenious, find some way to express yourself.

Even within the confines of the most rigid pastor's determination, the power and grace of the wedding ritual work their mystery, and your wedding will be beautiful. If it can't be all the personal statement you would like, it is, at least, testimony to your maturity which makes the best of a situation and realizes the essential value of the sacrament.

Indeed why get married in a church at all? We have been to lovely, small, very community-feeling weddings celebrated by a priest, properly registered, and performed in homes and outdoors (although chancery guidelines do not generally approve such settings). "Wherever there are two or three gathered together in my name, I am in their midst." Christ, of course, was there, and the atmosphere was exquisitely conducive to the feeling of closeness which the bride and groom wished to convey. The reception followed the Mass in unbroken feasting, a psychological and theatrically satisfying situation. And yet, perhaps some of the theology of marriage was missing which understands the wedding liturgy as part of the public worship of the Church and the marriage sacrament as a sign of Christ's love for the Church, which he created and has promised to sustain and does not abandon even when it seems to depart from his second law of love.

For most couples no serious conflicts arise. Minor points can be negotiated and accepted. Many pastors recognize that helping a couple develop a wedding ceremony relevant to them and within the general rubric of the Church renews a couple's faith in their Church at a time when they are making important future decisions together. These priests make every effort to understand and accommodate a culture that may be different from their own.

In fact, most pastors are delighted to see signs of life in a couple who care enough about the importance of their wedding ritual to want to bring to it their own thoughtful participation. Too many approach the ceremony with the idea that the priest marries them according to some ecclesiastical pattern which requires only their nervous presence and their promise and find it somehow frightening to analyze the ritual. Maybe they don't want to think too much about what they are doing. There are far too many couples (not you) who never read the new Rite of Marriage before they hear it on their big day, but the rite was designed to be read and thought about and worked with long prior to the ceremony.

If you will be married in a church where you are known and particularly if you are fortunate enough to be married in a church where you will continue to worship — the ideal choice — then you should be especially eager to include the parish community in your wedding plans.

Some parishes have made great efforts to help their brides and grooms recognize that their new married relationship is of special importance to the life of the community. In the weeks before their ceremony, the couple are prayed for during the general intercessions, perhaps even introduced. The parish liturgy committee has designed banners and vestments and gestures for use during a wedding ceremony. Someone at the church will coordinate a sharing of flowers among couples married around the same time. Following an idea presented by George B. Wilson, S.J., in *Worship* magazine and promulgated by Rev. Robert Hovda in his *Manual of Celebration,* a representative married couple of the parish is appointed to be present on the altar during the wedding ceremony and takes part in the greeting and homily and reception of vows for the purpose of making it apparent that married couples form a welcome "order" within the church and among society at large fruitful for their growth. You might even come to feel that it is appropriate to your situation that you be married during a regularly scheduled Sunday Mass.

Ask how your parish is assisting its couples and make use of what they are doing and, if it isn't much, start something! When the commentator opened the Prayer of the Faithful to the congregation's petitions, one couple rose, announced they would be married in that church in a few weeks, and asked the community to pray for them.

Formal and Informal

All weddings have a certain formality, and around them has grown up a vast amount of etiquette, at one time or another appropriate to the way people lived. Familiarity with this etiquette is useful and a look through Emily Post or Amy Vanderbilt and the guides in the various brides' magazines is recommended. You may opt for all of it, little of it, or none of it, but tradition-honored etiquette has a comforting security that frees you to dwell on other things. It is also useful to know what you have rejected so that it is done out of choice and not ignorance and doesn't become a cause of misunderstanding within the family. Probably no matter how independent your wedding you, and especially your mother, have in mind certain things that "ought" to be. More than the religious ceremony is ritual; there is certain valuable ritual to the preparation for a wedding celebration and to the reception afterward.

One couple, who played their preparation successfully by ear and non-conformism, found that reading a "who pays for what" list might have been constructive after all. She and her mother kept expecting to hear from the groom's mother about plans for a rehearsal dinner party. In the bride's experience the parents of the groom "always" did this. In his section of the country, there was no such tradition. A perusal of the rubrics may have been enlightening. It is the bride's responsibility, but in more and more areas it is becoming popular for the groom's family to make the gesture.

Strictly formal weddings with the bride in full white cathedral train regalia and the groom in cutaways fulfill many a bride's vision of herself — perhaps yours — and are particularly pleasing to some parents. Slightly less formal weddings with the groom in stroller jacket and striped trousers are probably the most common of all. The costuming of the couple sets the tone for the wedding and influences the design of all the supporting parts, up to a point. You need not be locked into every requirement under the heading "Formal Wedding." Many of today's couples mix and match and improvise cheerfully toward the total mood they wish their wedding to have. One strength of the revised rite is how well it works in the most formal or informal circumstances.

16

There is, in fact, a good deal of departure from traditional wedding clothes; your choice depends on what feels right and is the most fun for you. Mexican wedding dresses have a certain air of casualness, yet are within the bridal tradition of white gown-ness. Veils also are a statement that the bride cherishes tradition, but a crown of flowers is equally appropriate and more comfortable for the less formal bride. At any rate you'll want to dress up in some way, even if it's only a boutonniere in his buttonhole or buckskins and a flower lei. This day is different than other days and you are different from everyone else. Display it festively! Your guests, too, enjoy being part of the pageantry. It's fun to dress up.

Perhaps who pays for the wedding will significantly determine the taste of the celebration. Often an older bride and groom living away from home for several years and having many close friends unknown to their parents will assume total responsibility for their wedding.

The ingenuity of couples who try very hard to please themselves and their families and friends with events surrounding their wedding day is a tribute to everybody's understanding that weddings reflect commitment to past, present and future relationships. As one bride expressed it, "We were tempted to take our friends and our priest off to the woods and just get married, but I kept having flashes of our parents as our children's grandparents."

A Michigan couple participated wholeheartedly in a very formal traditional wedding with reception complete with father's business friends. A few evenings before they had celebrated their love in an engagement liturgy they designed themselves among a small community of friends with whom they expected to share future goals.

A New York couple reserved their wedding ceremony and the small reception following for themselves, their families and a few close friends, but attended elaborate engagement and post-nuptial parties given by their families.

Another mother for whom a sit-down dinner was "de rigueur" participated graciously and approvingly in her daughter's informal nuptial folk mass and the cake and champagne reception in the church hall, then took her friends and family out to dinner.

17

Choosing the Celebrant

Kurt Vonnegut, Jr., describing a real community, said it is ". . . made up of people who don't get along with each other because they don't have enough things in common. We have to struggle with that." Couples who truly wish their wedding to radiate love do struggle with that and find ways of creating an environment in which the grace of the sacrament can work the enduring success.

Perhaps more than anything else except your own attitude, your choice of the priest determines the flavor of your wedding. Of course *he* doesn't marry you. The wonderful fact that needs to be jubilantly shouted is that you confer the sacrament on each other by the exchange of your vows. Yet, the priest is your master of ceremonies and you and he are a production team that together bring out the full meaning of the wedding ritual.

It is wonderful if you can be married by a priest who is a good friend and with whom you share many ideas. If you don't know someone who is available, ask friends for suggestions. Before you approach the rectory to make the necessary arrangements for your marriage try and know which priest you wish to ask to marry you. Otherwise you are likely to be assigned the one who opens the door. Priests, like all of us, have different talents. As the American Bishops Committee on the Liturgy declared, "Good worship depends heavily upon the way a celebrant presides at liturgy, [for] good celebrants foster and nourish faith; poor celebrants weaken and destroy faith," and some priests are better at bringing us together than others. For your wedding it is of tremendous liturgical value for you to have a priest who has the gift of communication. Look for him. And, if family affection prescribes the choice of a dear friend who mumbles, consider concelebrants, bringing them together before your ceremony and tactfully steering each to the contribution he can make best.

The new Rite of Marriage lays particular stress on the role of a warm and friendly celebrant and encourages him to depart from formula and welcome the couple in his own well chosen words which express the joy the Church shares with the couple. The homily the priest gives will underline for those present the witness of the sacrament as *you* understand

18

and hope to live it. In the clear and simple way that he invites your vows and speaks the blessings and prayers, the priest can increase for you and your guests your awareness of the love and faithfulness expected of husband and wife and the divine and human help that is available to you. The priest can also graphically illustrate that the consent which you exchange is the visible sign of the sacrament by withdrawing himself from the central action at appropriate moments so that it becomes obvious to all that you are indeed the ministers of your marriage contract.

If he is properly exercising his pastoral responsibilities the priest will work with you in deciding among the many options provided for in the rite and will help you develop signs and gestures in your wedding that have liturgical significance and are best suited to you and your guests. He will offer for your decision his pet creative ideas from his own understanding of marriage and weddings he has celebrated and will make every effort to fulfill yours. He can also open doors for you if you want to be married in a church other than your own.

A section in the General Instruction of the Roman Missal bears quoting, though its reference is not specifically to weddings:

> The pastoral effectiveness of a celebration depends in great measure on choosing readings, prayers and songs which correspond to the needs, spiritual preparation and attitude of the participants. . . . In planning the celebration the priest should consider the spiritual good of the assembly rather than his own desires. . . .

If this dictum is true for all liturgies, it is especially important for the marriage ritual. As the official introduction to the rite wisely points out, weddings bring people to church (including the couple) who ordinarily are seldom seen there. Your wedding could influence the "turn on" or "turn off."

In addition to the spiritual empathy he offers you, the priest is your guide on a practical level. He will steer you through the pre-nuptial investigation which seeks to make certain that you are, according to civil and canon law, free to marry and are making the decision of your own informed will. You might be prepared for the detail and personal nature of some of the questions, like your intention regarding birth control, but almost always the investigation is painlessly routine. In some dioceses two people who have known you a sufficient amount of time also answer questions. The priest will also know the status on publicly announcing bans, a practice waning, but not yet abandoned. He will further advise you of the necessary records you will need to furnish the church where you plan to be married. These include copies of your certificates of baptism and confirmation. If you don't have copies, they can easily be obtained from the church where the event took place. You'll also be informed of civil requirements like blood tests and, of course, the marriage license. If your priest is not associated with the church where he is celebrating your marriage, he will need permission from that church.

Remember that you should give a money gift to the priest who officiates, but a close friend may prefer your gratefully chosen personal gift. The church will expect a fee and often stipulates a specific one.

At the request of a priest friend with a reputation for presiding at creative weddings and often sought out by friends of friends of friends who want him to work his magic at their ceremony, I offer this thought. As the priest has a ministerial responsibility to you, you have a most human responsibility to him. Don't use the priest. He is neither producer nor performer, but participant. Your day works honestly and his joy in it increases in proportion to how much you have opened yourselves to him and made him a part of your continuing community. If your priest is just brought in for the "how to," you and he are cheated of a most beautiful encounter of soul.

What About Attendants?

Other people are important participants in your wedding ceremony also. The tradition of bridesmaids and groomsmen is an ancient and practical one that has lost a bit of its original dramatic flavor. The groom no longer needs his cohorts to help him steal the bride! Still it is a privilege to be asked to share a wedding ceremony in this special way and it is a good feeling for you to be surrounded by friends with whom you are especially close.

20

It is a pretty picture, too, to see the brightly dressed girls and smartly dressed men walk down the aisle, frame the altar and grace the reception table.

However, many couples, in changing the strictly traditional treatment of their wedding ceremony, are also changing the role of attendants, and you may wish to examine your attitude toward attendants in light of their experiences. It is often very hard from among all your friends to select only a few who will stand out on that day as being distinctly special to you. There is a nostalgia about your wedding that looks back to old friends, some of whom realistically have drifted away from you. There is also the wish, because your wedding looks toward the future you will share together, to include couples whom you expect to see often. Then, too, you may want to invite brothers and sisters of each other who will definitely be a part of your future life. All this could result in quite a parade marching down the aisle or some hurt feelings among the non-marchers.

It is sometimes very wise and sensitive to have only one attendant each as your official witness and to give all the people you invite to the wedding the feeling that they are there because they are special to you and have a specific participation in your ceremony: they are, indeed, all called upon to witness your promise to each other.

You may begin to think, too, that dressing your friends all alike or the girls in varying shades of the same costume blurs their individuality. They are, of course, each very different, each has a different relationship with you, and each has something distinctive that he or she could bring to your ceremony. Often the attendants strike an attractive but passive pose throughout your wedding. They are so many props, a uniform chorus line dressing the stage for the stars.

Not that a wedding doesn't have many of the characteristics of a stage production. There are the invitations as tickets, the altar as stage, parents as backers, guests as audience, the bride and groom in leading roles, the priests and attendants as supporting cast, the stage set, the costuming, the script, and it all comes together better if everyone knows and understands his lines and it is rehearsed. It is far from scandal to think of a wedding this way. Religious ritual has always had historical association with drama, but a drama that is participatory, vital, symbolic and festive. The "bride" and "groom" are also themselves.

If you do have attendants make them feel like more than background. Give them something to do. Or, think about having no attendants as such, but asking friends with special gifts to use their talents before, during, or after your wedding ceremony to the enhancement of your day. As Charles Reich observed:

> ... one of the natural urges of man is to perform for his friends by playing a musical instrument, singing, dancing, acting or cooking. It is a mode of communicating and relating that is very different from conversation and to judge by primitive societies at least as important as conversation. Passive culture almost completely denies performance ... [And your wedding is anything but passive!]

A seamstress friend or relative may make the bride's dress, the groom a colorful tie or shirt, and the priest's vestments. If there is a little old wine maker in the group, he can make the wine for the Eucharist. Someone may offer to bake the bread. Although you won't want to establish talent as the sole criterion for those who will deliver the readings, don't pass up someone who will be especially good at this. You do want your guests to have the full impact of the words. A lector to introduce the parts of the Mass may be useful, particularly if many of the guests are non-Catholics.

Perhaps there is a dancer among your friends whose dancing would not be so much gimmick, but a real liturgical contribution. Maybe a potter could make the offertory dishes. Probably you have friends who sing and those who play musical instruments. Possibly a friend can design and make your rings. Perhaps there is someone who would like to take over the flower arrangements for you, not just ordering the usual from the florist, but finding a garden.

Among your friends there are certainly banner and poster makers, if this is going to be part of the scene for your wedding. There are balloon blower-uppers, too, if you wish this note of festivity. And it helps if the best man or someone has an organized mind, keeping track of marriage licenses, rings, fees, luggage, etc.

22

Programs and Invitations

Whatever the type wedding you plan, traditional (but with your own stamp) or very new, it adds to the ease of everyone's participation if he has a program, a detailed guide, with which to follow your ceremony. This is particularly important because there are times when you will wish the whole congregation to make a response. Of course, there are paper missalettes which you can buy and these are useful, but if you plan special songs and adaptions and additions to the rite, you'll want to design your own. Ask a friend to help. Try not to be mimeographing at 2 a.m. the morning of the wedding.

For many guests a copy of the entire liturgy is a thoughtful souvenir of the wedding and couples have paid particular attention to this. It might have a handsome cover and open as a book, easier to deal with than single sheets stapled together. One Boston couple included pictures and an introduction giving a brief background of their meeting and coming to love one another and a biography of their witnesses, musicians, parents and celebrant. Reading the booklet gave everyone something to do while waiting for the bride and increased his anticipation for the coming ceremony.

Many couples use the booklet as their opportunity to greet and thank their guests and remark on the day's particular meaning to them:

> Without a community, sacrament is diminished. This is a copy of our marriage ceremony and the eucharistic celebration of it. We hope that reading it will bring you joy and remind you of the part you played as witness to us. —*Kenneth and Katherine Clancy-Hepburn*

Some find this their chance to consciousness-raise with a poem or personal statement or secular reading, perhaps one which they were unable to make part of the ceremony.

A Long Island couple included their planned reception toasts to their parents and friends.

A friend may also help you design your invitations (and one with legible handwriting can be enlisted to address them), for invitations are another thing that have departed from the

23

letter of tradition. Many couples wish right from the start to set a theme of warmth and welcome for their ceremony, and they send invitations which illustrate their attitude. Among our collection is a delightful silkscreen of a wavy yellow line and a wavy blue line that meet in a bright green balloon. Another is a linoleum block print of the wedding symbol, the Greek Christ sign and interlocking rings, against the background of a dove, symbol of love and peace. Some are Corita-like with joyful epithets expressing the couple's idea of their day. One favorite includes on the cover the e. e. cummings poem which begins:

> i thank you God for most this amazing
> day: for the leaping greenly spirits of trees
> and a blue true dream of sky; and for everything
> which is natural which is infinite which is yes*

The couple used a little literary license and changed the "i" to "we."

It is also possible to order a design cover from a commercial printer and inside to have printed your own personal message.

The self-composed invitations we have received have emphasized the great joy of the union and the desire of the family to have us share in it. Most of these invitations have followed tradition and been issued in the name of the bride's parents: Below is one example:

> Please join our family on Saturday, June the fifth, nineteen hundred and seventy-one, at one-thirty o'clock in the Chapel of the Immaculate Heart of Mary, Santa Fe, New Mexico, when we joyfully celebrate the marriage of our daughter, Gerlinda Annette, with Grant Alden Somerville. Your witness will mean so much to us all. —*Fred and Cleo Gallegos*

In the European tradition the parents of the bride issue the invitation to the wedding and reception, but there is included an announcement by the groom's parents of their son's plan to be married, thus indicating their approval. A Cincinnati couple, very close to their parents, designed a charming

---

* e.e. cummings, "i thank you god for most this amazing," from *Poems 1923-1954.* Used by permission of Harcourt Brace Jovanovich, Inc.

invitation expressing the idea that the two families were delighted to be joined by the marriage of their children. The invitation was a small booklet: on the cover was a picture of the bride's parents striking an old-fashioned pose in a quaint, ornate frame; the second page showed the groom's parents; the engaged couple smiled out from the third page. On the last page both families announced their pleasure in the upcoming wedding and the bride's parents issued an invitation ". . . to the Nuptial Mass and reception celebrating this most holy and happy day."

Another Cincinnati couple expanded the above invitation idea, following a custom happily gaining advocates all across the country. Both sets of parents gave the wedding and the invitation announced their mutual involvement.

Formal engraved invitations are sacred to other parents and to many brides. Study your guest list. If you're being married among your mutual friends and few of your parents' friends are being invited, send your free-spirited invitations, perhaps arranging for formal announcements, sent the day of the wedding, to go to your parents' friends who are not invited. If your list, however, includes many of your parents' friends, and especially if your wedding is very formal, you may want to give in gracefully on this point. Consider, though, the eventual pride of the mother of the groom who cringed at but did not try to overrule her future daughter-in-law's invitation design, and was all set to offer apologies for the departure from traditional etiquette. As soon as the first mail was in, she got a call from a friend who said, "I really feel they want me at this wedding. I'm looking forward to it."

WEDDING MUSIC

One reason for the new found fun in weddings has to be the music. Alive! Embracing! Communicating! What *this* wedding is all about is often told in sound and song. The lyrics coax our understanding; the rhythm invites our response. Who doesn't feel a part of the wedding when the music demands he really listen or the melody irresistibly urges him to sing and the beat has his body moving. Music lifts all our moods to a shared moment. "We are one in the Spirit; we are one in the Lord." It brings us together to "try and love one another right now."

Traditional or Modern?

In the very near past the majority of couples planning their wedding simply told the church organist to "play the usual," only occasionally knowledgeable enough themselves in the approved sacred music to dare suggest a particular piece. Sometimes the results were magnificent! The church organist, a superb musician, playing a superior instrument, arranged for a fine soloist, maybe even a well-trained choir, and selected among the music of the masters, pieces which swelled the heart, highlighted the important moments of the

26

Sing a new song to the LORD;
  sing to the LORD, all men on earth.
Sing to the LORD and bless his name,
  Proclaim his triumph day by day.
  . . . and dance in his honour. . .
                              —*Psalm 96*

ceremony and got you out in resounding purpose and triumph.

More often the poor underpaid or volunteer organist did his or her best with a limited music education and an inferior instrument. The result was, at worst, deadly, lulling us into missing half the action; at best, adequate, but dull, the music creating no involvement and no memory whatsoever, simply there.

Today, with music an integral part of their culture, arising from the way they live, expressing so well what they feel and fear and understand and hope, few young couples, thank God, can leave the music for their wedding to someone else's decision. The results are, at worst, noisy, not very good art, disconcerting to some guests, yet withal personal and exuberant; at best, impressive contemporary art, joyous, enveloping, telling and truly religious.

Of course, if you really are into E. Power Biggs and have access to the magnificent organ and skilled organist, you will want to treat your guests to the rich, ennobling, uplifting, unifying experience of traditional church music. The rare and fortunate church which has this would probably preclude any other type of wedding music anyway. You'll enjoy replacing the Bridal Chorus from Wagner's *Lohengrin* with something less often heard and more suitable. (Anyone who knows *Lohengrin* wouldn't want this tragic bedroom fiasco in their wedding, and often it is not permitted.) You'll also have fun making your substitution for the overdone recessional music, Mendelssohn's "Wedding March." Peal the carillons! "With trumpet and echoing horn acclaim the presence of the LORD our king" (Psalm 98).

If you're not into Mr. Biggs and company and/or your church's organ and its master or mistress have never done anything to make you feel remotely closer to God, then you'll want to exploit the type music you do like and understand as well as the musicians you know who can play and sing it well.

Some protocol governs doing your own thing. When your church has an organist you're not using, you are usually responsible for his fee, or, at least, a portion of it. You may also be required to submit your music selections and their instruments and musicians to a review by the church music director, if there is one, or to the pastor.

Many are, at least, tolerant, and, not surprisingly, sometimes more so when their own church music program is quite good. Then they are apt to recognize the genuine musicianship of "popular" artists: the complicated structures of former Beatles McCartney, Lennon, and Harrison, to name the most obvious; the poetry in the lyrics of Bob Dylan, Paul Simon, Neil Young, and Pete Seeger at his best. Such churches give generous interpretation to the words of the Constitution on the Sacred Liturgy, realizing that music imposed has no liturgical value but that "from the people" can be prayer:

> In certain parts of the world, especially mission lands, there are peoples who have their own musical traditions, and these play a great part in their religious and social life. For this reason due importance is to be attached to their music, and a suitable place is to be given to it, not only in forming their attitude towards religion, but also in adapting worship to their native genius, as indicated in Art. 39 and 40. [i.e. the liturgy should adapt to the culture and traditions of people].

More and more churches are better than tolerant of your music choices. Perhaps their folk and rock masses inspired them. Maybe their folk group will perform them. If you're among a lucky few your parish's liturgy committee has a solid music program which offers you broad suggestions for popular folk, soul-gospel, country, rock and jazz, as well as traditional religious music, appropiate to weddings, and is eager to add your selections to their collection.

Most typically, however, you find yourself the victim or the benefactor of the musical limbo in which too many churches languish: a repertoire of religious hymns and pseudo-folk songs of the da da/da da/da da/da dum variety supported by a sluggish organ and transient guitarists and song leaders.

Match this so-called "religious" music to the quality and content of that of some secular artists, many of whom take their inspiration directly from the Bible, certainly from the commandments of Christ. These are God's children using the talents he gave them in praise of what he created and he taught. Of course, it is religious. Often "popular" music says it so much better than its limping theme equivalent in arrangements specifically designed for the church market. It is less shallow and sentimental, stronger, gutsier, more graphic, more deeply concerned with relationships among and between God and this man and these men and all men, more seeking of commitment. Compare Paul Simon's "Bridge Over Troubled Water," Burt Bacharach and Hal David's "What the World Needs Now Is Love," Pete Seeger's interpretation of the third chapter of Ecclesiastes "Turn! Turn! Turn! (To everything there is a season . . .)," Arlo Guthrie's "Valley to Pray," Paul Stookey's recording of an old song of obscure origin:

Wedding Song

He is now to be among you at the calling of your hearts,
Rest assured this troubadour is acting on His part.
The union of your spirits here has caused Him to remain,
For wher'ever two or more of you are gathered in His name
There is love . . . There is love.

Well, a man shall leave his mother and a woman
    leave her home,

They shall travel on to where the two shall be as one.
As it was in the beginning is now and 'til the end,
Woman draws her life from man and gives it back again
And there is love . . . There is love.

Well, then what's to be the reason for becoming
   man and wife?
Is it love that brings you here, or love that brings you life?
For if loving is the answer, then who's the giving for?
Do you believe in something that you haven't seen before?
Oh, there's love . . . Oh, there's love.

The marriage of your spirits here has caused Him to remain,
For wher'ever two or more of you are gathered in His name
There is love . . . There is love.*

When you're on your own to find your songs and your
musicians, the freedom is terrific if you're really in the scene;
a challenge if you know vaguely what you like and don't like,
but music isn't your forte.

   If you're among the latter, don't surrender this important part of your liturgical contribution to your ceremony to
the lackluster of the parish; seek help. Find out which
Catholic and non-Catholic churches in your area are doing
exciting things in their music programs. Perhaps you can use
their artists or they can suggest a group to you. Talk to
friends more involved with music than you are. You may find
the talent you need among them or on a local college
campus, at the local seminary, monastery, or music school.
Good music is out there somewhere and available to your
persistence.

How to Make the Music Work

Good music! Whose criteria? Isn't it all a question of taste
and how tastes differ? To a degree, but couples in whose
wedding celebrations music has really worked, have generally
agreed on a few objective criteria for their selection:

   First, how stands this music within the knowledgeable
music community of which it is a type? In other words, if it
is "church music" what does the Pius X School of Liturgical
Music think of it as opposed to Father McKenzie "writing the

* "Wedding Song" (There Is Love) © 1971 by Public Domain Foundation, Inc. Used
by permission.

30

words of a sermon no one will hear."

Or, if "popular" music, how does it impress music critics as opposed to your sister. The rigid standards of criterion one, however, must be yielding to criterion two and, above all, criterion three.

Second, how appropriate are *these* words and *this* sound to what you're trying to say at this particular moment in your wedding? It may be a wonderful song, perfect for some liturgies, yet not relate to the circumstances of your marriage or those of any wedding. Resist the temptation to fit it in somewhere just because you like the song. Enjoy it at the reception. It may be a great song for a wedding entrance, but not at the offertory. Consciously or unconsciously sensitive couples have appreciated the artistic and psychological truth that "Sacred music is to be considered the more holy in proportion as it is more closely connected with the liturgical action" (Constitution on the Sacred Liturgy). The music must support what is being done by the bridal couple at the altar, reinforce it, underline it, illuminate it, hang a garland around its neck. No matter how beautiful and entertaining, if it distorts or distracts from the central theme and the liturgical activity of the moment, forget it.

In the chapters and Appendix following, specific songs and music are suggested as models for specific actions of the liturgy. Generally you will want music before your entrance, at your entrance, after the vows, during the offertory, at communion and at your exit. Too much of a good thing (noise and numbers) will leave the impression of your wedding as one great sound experience: "less is more."

I hesitate to make a comment about the hard-rock sound because I don't know it very well, but I have never seen it work well at a wedding. I have seen it fall sadly on its face, simply virtuoso performance, overwhelming the ceremony, making guests uncomfortable. I suppose it might work if almost all the guests are Consciousness III. Few weddings are like that. Nowhere more than in your wedding music is your harmony with the community achieved and sustained. If the music does not bring together the people you invite to share the celebration, then it is not for your day.

On the other hand, a very soft-rock sound (sometimes borrowing hard-rock lyrics) seems capable of bridging the generation gap. I have seen older couples whose ideas of wedding music strayed little from Bach's "Jesu, Joy of Man's Desiring" lured into appreciative response at a ceremony which took its music chiefly from the rock musical *Godspell*. The wedding pair employed a three-piece combo, two guitarists and a string-bass player with tambourine and recorder, singing themselves and accompanying a vocalist.

Third, how well can this music and song be performed at your wedding? Better something simple, well done, than a complicated failure. Experimentation is valuable in liturgy, but your wedding is more valuable, one-shot, and of lasting memory. In some liturgical space a single musician can handle most music very well. Other liturgical space and music selections require more musicians. A soloist can enhance one song, another calls for a group. If a friend really can play the organ, the guitar, the recorder, the flute, or whatever, or really sing, accept his offer or nudge him into making one. If not, it's well worth while paying for talent.

Community Singing

At several points in the liturgy you'll want all your friends to join together in song. Nothing gives them quite the same feeling of participation and well-being. However, your weddings guests, drawn from a cross section of two lives, are unlikely to be a group who has sung together before or even knows the same music. The song you select must be thoroughly familiar to diverse types, the melody simple and catchy, the music enticing, toe tapping and body swaying even. Songs like the "Amen" from *Lilies of the Field*, "Kumbaya," "He's Got the Whole World in His Hands," personalized with your names, and "Day by Day" from *Godspell* lend themselves gracefully to certain moments and "on-the-spot" learning if they're not already known. There is little that sounds worse and makes more obvious the fact that your guests are not together, than imposing a song on untutored, reluctant, fumbling congregational singing. Give the more difficult songs to a soloist or small group. Listening, too, is participation. And the balance of the big sound, the soft sound and silence is welcome.

Many couples have successfully brought off the performance of a great deal of community participation. They have done it with careful preparation and a knowledge of their guests' experience and willingness to learn. Maybe you know that most of your friends participate in folk masses and most of these masses share the same music you plan to utilize, perhaps chiefly because of your guests' familiarity with it. (Even the da da/da dum music can have value.)

Probably many of your guests will be getting together at parties before your wedding where you can take the opportunity to introduce songs and rehearse them. At least your attendants (use them! give them something to do!), your families, and your priest ("if father is doing it, it must be all right") can be coached in the words and rhythm. The fact that some don't have great voices, but still are giving their all will only stimulate your more inhibited guests to contribute.

Finally, while your guests, supplied with programs containing the words, are seated waiting for the ceremony to begin, a song leader can teach the more easily and quickly learned songs, refrains, psalm responses, and Sanctus. Indeed, such a warmup session is a delightful mood setter for the coming event. Have your song leader explain how meaningful everyone's singing out will be to the two of you. By the time you arrive your guests will have decided they have something real to give to you, and that's a good feeling. Also have the song leader explain that this is planned and you will be arriving in about ten minutes. Otherwise a few guests will be distracted by the nervous thought that this is stalling for time while someone finds the groom.

The placement of your musicians and singers helps, too. To the side so they don't upstage you, but up front where they can be seen and where their enthusiasm will be contagious.

What we all "catch" from the music of your wedding is a share in your joy.

THE ENTRANCE RITE

Setting the Scene

Your wedding celebration is about to begin. You are dressed in your most festive clothes, your parents are masking emotions of love and joy and memory behind a busy facade, your guests are excitedly arriving. The church is in readiness, decorated with the things you have thought important to create the atmosphere you wish your wedding day to have:

. . . gay colored balloons are attached to the pew ends or seats which form the aisle.

. . . the runner is a long bright banner painted and sewn by friends: Welcome Anne and Brian. . . welcome Mom and Dad, Muvie and Papa, Grandma Dodd, Friends!. . . walk in the way of the Lord. . . clap your hands with gladness. . . "this is the birth day of life and of love and wings;

34

. . . There was a wedding, first of all, in the garden of Paradise. It was the crowning point of creation. Through six long "days" God had worked up to it, prepared for it, taken great pains with it. Finally, he gave man and woman to each other and human love was born. God saw what he had done was very good, and he rejoiced within himself at what he had wrought. He blessed the man and woman and rested from his labors. . .

—*Eugene S. Geissler*

and of the gay great happening illimitably earth"*. . . "write me as one that loves his fellow men."

. . . banners flank the altar:. . . This is the day which the Lord has made; let us rejoice and be glad in it (Psalm 118:24). . . For all things are yours, the world or life or death or the present or the future, all are yours (1 Corinthians 3:21-22). . . From this time forth I make you hear new things, hidden things which you have not known (Isaiah 48:6).

. . . multi-hued flowers are in abundance.

Or, maybe quieter than this. White flowers, a theme of yellow or pink, cornflowers and daisies, white runner, no balloons. Candles, few flowers. No flowers. Your choice. Simple, lovely.

---

* e.e. cummings, "i thank you god for most this amazing," from *Poems 1923-1954*. Used by permission of Harcourt Brace Jovanovich, Inc.

The entrance rite is prelude to the Mass. It stirs the thoughts of the community in common direction, sets the theme of the day, establishes an environment, encourages a mood. This first encounter with those you have invited is your opportunity to prepare others to see your marriage as you see it.

One fun way couples have found to do this is to start before the official rite begins. Perhaps a reception first at home with punch, a wandering troubadour, and a chance for your guests to meet and chat with one another. Then a procession through the streets to the church. Too confusing? Your home is too distant for walking? Then if the church has a garden, a basement will do; why not a small reception there first? Your guests enter the church then in a bond of fellowship and with a party feeling.

At the door your attendants or friends and any children present can welcome each guest with the program and a flower or a button stamped with a smile or maybe saying ". . . love our so right."* Unless you are planning the grand entrance or are convinced that bad luck stalks the groom who even glimpses the bride, the two of you can mingle with your friends.

You and all your attendants (yes, the girls, too! especially the graciousness and charm of the girls) might take people to their seats. The tradition of ushering is a warm one, symbolizing the care you have for those invited. They are special.

Music, lively, happy, jubilant, can fill the church as the guests arrive. Once seated, the warm-up session begins, rehearsing the songs you wish everyone to sing.

And then perhaps a solo or reading (the one which opens this chapter, maybe) of real meaning to settle everyone down and focus their thoughts. Now might be the time you wish a commentator to step forward and give an introduction such as one a friend delivered for this couple:

John and Simone are very happy to be able to share with you the celebration of their marriage. Their own love for each other has grown out of the love which

---

* e.e. cummings, "love our so right," from *Poems 1923-1954*. Used by permission of Harcourt Brace Jovanovich, Inc.

36

they have found first in their homes and then among the community of friends and associates they have lived and worked with. Since their marriage is but an extension and a continuation of those deep friendships, they wish that you, as a community of friends, witness and bless their union.

They also hope that this shared experience will deepen their own awareness as well as yours of the need for their love to be set within the broader context of the community's needs and hopes.

Paraphrasing the words of Antoine de Saint-Exupery, they wish to find and grow their love not by sitting and gazing into one another's eyes, but in looking outward together in the same direction to that which best serves the peace and sustains the hope of you their community of friends.

So it is that John and Simone wish you to share in the joy of their mutual love. But they wish, too, to share in the movement, history and hope of the community of man which by our love we continually create.

In one part of the ceremony we will hear readings chosen to help express the sentiments which they hope to carry into their marriage. The exchange of vows will be followed by two ritual acts: the greeting of peace and the breaking of bread.

These two gestures symbolize within the Christian community the reconciliation and unity which all men seek.

Simone and John invite you to give the greeting and share in the common meal which express for them the ideals of peace, thanksgiving and unity of which they wish their own marriage to be a sign and a sacrament.

Going Up the Aisle

At last, here comes the bride! You may choose a traditional processional, improvise your own, or adapt one from the suggestions below. Muse on the fact that the traditional processional had its origin in the days of dowries when marriages were arranged by parents for social and political reasons and the sheltered bride was handed over to a groom she knew slightly or not at all. Doubtless not the case with the two of you. The official rite dictates no particular method of entrance, but it does make two happy suggestions: that the priest greet the bride and groom at the church door and that both bride and groom accompanied by their parents and their witnesses proceed to the altar.

For example, the priest says from the altar, "I am going now to the door of the church to greet Grant and Gigi in the name of the Church and in your name. Let us stand and sing our welcome to them." The congregation begins:

Enter, Rejoice and Come In

Enter, rejoice and come in
Enter, rejoice and come in

Chorus
Today will be a joyful day,
Enter, rejoice and come in.

Open your hearts to the Lord,
Open your hearts to the Lord. *Chorus*

Open your hearts to all men,
Open your hearts to all men. *Chorus*

Sing Hallelu. . . . . . ia,
Sing Hallelu. . . . . . ia. *Chorus*

The priest, after a few warm words to the couple, leads in the groom escorted by his parents and best man and other attendants if any, and the bride escorted by her parents, official witness, and attendants.

The bride and her family and the groom and his family may come from separate rooms and meet at the door if they wish to preserve some "no see" tradition. In an evening Mass the bride might exchange her wedding bouquet for a candle. The others, too, might carry lighted candles into a darkened church. The couple then light the altar candles with their own. The bride and groom kiss their parents and leave them

38

and join each other before the altar. Each may say aloud or quietly to his or her own parents a few spontaneous or personally prepared words of thank you:

Thank you Mom and Dad for bringing me to this day. We have learned love from you and hope in our marriage to always return it to you.

It makes sense if official witnesses join your parents in their seats, stepping forward only at appropriate moments. If you will be comfortable doing it, you may choose to sit facing your friends, symbolizing your community with them and the fact that you are the ministers of this sacrament. If this seems awkward to you, arrange the chairs so you are sideways and can be seen. Turning your back to everyone with the priest towering over you suggests this is a private act and gives the impression that marriage is something done to you and not by you.

You may not wish the congregation to sing your wedding welcome, choosing instead a solo or group singing of a song like that which Joan Baez and Mahalia Jackson have recorded, the popular Protestant hymn, "Just a Closer Walk with Thee." And if you wish, even if the rest of your wedding repertoire is not classical, you may elect a traditional resounding instrumental processional like that credited to Purcell, the heralding "Trumpet Voluntary in D." Whatever your decision you won't creep staidly past your guests, unseeing. Enter with verve and warmth, embracing your friends in your delight at being here.

As another entrance variation your attendants might, instead of processing down the aisle, come out on the altar with the priest to greet you. A few couples have eschewed a processional altogether. One bride and groom came out on the altar before the priest, addressed a welcome to the congregation, then called to the priest and their attendants to "come, witness our marriage." Another followed the priest who gave a very short introduction, then turned at the sound of a bell rung by the couple:

Celebrant: Maureen and Tom, what do you ask of this church and this company?
Groom: We ask you, Father, in the name of the Church to

witness and bless the marriage promise we intend to make with one another.

Bride: We ask this company, our parents, our family, and our friends who have come to be with us today, to *really* be with us, to share our joy, recognize our love, approve our marriage, and pray for us always.

You have arrived. You are not afraid to look at one another. Hold hands. Smile.

Preliminary Prayers

In the usual Order of the Mass, the introductory rites begin:

Entrance Antiphon (stand)

The following is the most frequently used, but another from Scripture may appeal to you more. It may be recited (as below) or sung, probably as a solo, together with Psalm 127:

All: May the God of Israel join you together; and may He be with you, Who was merciful to two only children; and now, O Lord, make them bless You more fully. (P.T. Alleluia, alleluia.) Tobit 7:15, 8:19

The Sign of the Cross (stand)

Celebrant: In the name of the Father, and of the Son, and of the Holy Spirit.

All: Amen.

Greeting

The priest then greets the people in the words of one of three options given him in the official Order of the Mass or, preferably, and as is encouraged in the rite, in his own friendly and descriptive words which relate specifically to marriage and to this marriage:

Welcome to today. This is a great day. Today we celebrate the Mass which Christ has given his bride, the Church, as a sign and a promise of his love for us and his

union with us. Today we celebrate another promise of
love, another sign of union, the sacrament of marriage.
This is a wedding day — a man and a woman, a groom
and a bride, within God's promise to us, now make their
promise to each other. Today is very much like any
other wedding day, but it is also like no wedding you
have ever known before because today is Anne and
Brian's wedding day. And those of us who have watched
this unique romance grow know that never again could a
couple love as Anne and Brian love, never again will a
couple serve God quite as Anne and Brian serve him,
never again will a couple have the children together that
Anne and Brian will have. The Church is the spouse of
Christ and we are the Church. Today Anne and Brian
become each the spouse of the other and you and I are
their witnesses. Let us be grateful for this Mass and for
Anne and Brian. Both show us there does exist love
strong enough to promise love.

    The Lord be with you.
All: And also with you.

One priest linked his greeting appropriately and beautifully
with the penitential rite which follows it:

> We have come to celebrate the Banquet of Life
> which Christ has given us in the Eucharist and to
> witness the Feast of Love which Nancy and John
> are to share in marriage. Let us begin by
> reminding ourselves that that love must be a part
> of our lives, and let us kneel to confess that we
> have not loved enough.

The Penitential Rite (kneel)

The rite which followed the greeting immediately above
continued with the prayer of each guest:

> All: Father, your Son has shown us how to love
> and invites us to love one another
> as he loves us. We confess that our lives
> have not been a fulfillment of this.

We have been proud and selfish, impatient with others,
and all too accommodating to ourselves.
We have not trusted enough in your love
and in the love of each other.

We have not been open with each other, afraid
to take the chance that in loving we may not be
loved in return.

There are times when we have had the opportunity
to make love for one another a reality, and
we have remained silent.

Father, pardon the unkind word,
the impatient gesture,
and the selfish deed.

Forgive our failure to become involved
in the needs of others.

Grant that we may walk always in your presence
so as to arrive at the fullness of life.*

Usually the priest chooses one of three optional forms for the penitential rite from the usual Order of the Mass. At the end of any form of the penitential rite the priest says:

**Celebrant: May almighty God have mercy on us,
forgive us our sins,
and bring us to everlasting life.
All: Amen.**

Kyrie

If it is possible to rehearse communal singing for this, there are many available arrangements, at least one consistent with the style music you have chosen. One groom and his musician friends composed their own arrangement: "Kyrie eleison, forgive us the love we have not shown." If it cannot be sung wholeheartedly, then it is recited:

**Celebrant: Lord, have mercy.
All: Lord, have mercy.**

---

* By Donald L. Cooke, S.J., from *The Experimental Liturgy Book,* ed. by Robert F.
Hoey, S.J., © 1969 by Herder and Herder.

Celebrant: Christ, have mercy.
     All: Christ, have mercy.
Celebrant: Lord have mercy.
     All: Lord, have mercy.

Gloria

Again, if it can be done well, this is lovely sung. If not it is
recited:

Celebrant: Glory to God in the highest,
     All: and peace to his people on earth.
              Lord God, heavenly King,
              almighty God and Father,
                 we worship you, we give you thanks.
              we praise you for your glory.
              Lord Jesus Christ, only Son of the Father,
              Lord God, Lamb of God,
              you take away the sin of the world:
                 have mercy on us;
              you are seated at the right hand of the Father:
                 receive our prayer.
              For you alone are the Holy One,
              you alone are the Lord,
              you alone are the Most High,
                 Jesus Christ,
                 with the Holy Spirit,
                 in the glory of God the Father. Amen.

Opening Prayer

The priest next slowly and clearly calls us to worship making
us aware once more of the celebration theme: this is *your*
wedding day:

Celebrant: Let us pray. (Silent reflection of all)

The official rite provides you and your priest with four
options for this prayer. Each one is slightly different. Read
them through carefully and decide which one you like best
and tell the priest the one you wish him to say:

Choice one

Father,
you have made the bond of marriage
a holy mystery,
a symbol of Christ's love for his Church
Hear our prayers for N. and N.
With faith in you and in each other
May they pledge their love today.
May their lives always bear witness
to the reality of that love.

Choice two

Father,
hear our prayers for N. and N.,
who today are united in marriage before your altar.
Give them your blessing,
and strengthen their love for each other.

Choice three

Almighty God,
hear our prayers for N. and N.,
who have come here today
to be united in the sacrament of marriage.
Increase their faith in you and in each other,
and through them bless your Church
    (with Christian children).

Choice four

Father,
when you created mankind
you willed that man and wife should be one.
Bind N. and N.
in the loving union of marriage;
and make their love fruitful
so that they may be living witnesses
to your divine love in the world.

All of the options end with the same prayer:

**We ask this
through our Lord Jesus Christ, your Son,
who lives and reigns with you
and the Holy Spirit,
one God, for ever and ever.**

If none of these options say exactly what you want them to say at this point in your Mass, talk it over with your priest. You may be able to adapt one or design one which tells it exactly as it is for you.

The Entrance Rite is over. Your guests know why they are here. In Christ and in community with one another, they are thinking with you, preparing with you, praying with you, and they are having a very good time.

THE LITURGY OF THE WORD

In this part of the Mass God speaks directly to you through the words he has caused to be written in Scripture. And you speak to your guests through the scriptures you choose to have read.

The options presented by the new rite are many: from among twenty-eight, you select three, one from the Old Testament, one from the letters of the Apostles to the early Church, and one from the Gospels. With your selections you sketch a picture of how you feel and want to feel about the marriage promise you are about to make. You may play a theme and variations with your choices, each of your selections illuminating from a slightly different angle the same point, the one most important to you, or you may choose three entirely different passages, each of which spotlights an aspect of marriage that you wish to be a part of your own.

Your guests are seated comfortably for the first two readings. The people you ask to read have been chosen because they are so close to you that you wish to honor them with a special part in your ceremony and because they can give the readings the clarity and emphasis they deserve. Dad might be a perfect choice, but some Dads are monotones.

When all things began, the Word already was.
The Word dwelt with God, and what God was, the
Word was. . . and that life was the light of men. . .
So the Word became flesh; he came to dwell among
us and we saw his glory. . . full of grace and truth.

—John 1

The Old Testament Readings

Your first reading is chosen from among the following eight
Old Testament options:

Choice one—GENESIS 1:26-28, 31a

Then God said, "Let us make man in our image and
likeness to rule the fish in the sea, the birds of heaven,
the cattle, all wild animals on earth, and all reptiles that
crawl upon the earth." So God created man in his own
image; male and female he created them. God blessed
them and said to them, "Be fruitful and increase, fill the
earth and subdue it, rule over the fish in the sea, the
birds of heaven, and every living thing that moves upon
the earth." So it was; and God saw all that he had made,
and it was very good.

If you are into horticulture you might also include verses 29
and 30:

God also said, "I give you all plants that bear seed
everywhere on earth, and every tree bearing fruit which
yields seed: they shall be yours for food."

One couple for whom ecology was and would be in their
marriage, a vital concern, stepped forward after this reading,

the groom as spokesman, to make their comment: "Seeing what man has done to the wonderful world he created, would God say now that 'it was very good?' Rachel Carson in her book *Silent Spring* writes a sequel to the story of creation":

> Then a strange blight crept over the area and everything began to change. Some evil spell had settled on the community: mysterious maladies swept the flocks of chickens; the cattle and sheep sickened and died. . . . There was a strange stillness. The birds, for example — where had they gone? . . . It was a spring without voices. . . . On the farms the hens brooded, but no chicks hatched. The farmers. . . were unable to raise any pigs — the litters were small and the young survived only a few days. The apple trees were coming into bloom but no bees droned among the blossoms, so there was no pollination and there would be no fruit. . . . No witchcraft, no enemy action had silenced the rebirth of new life in this stricken world. The people had done it themselves.*

Choice two—GENESIS 2:18-24

In the passage above "man" is mankind, male and female, both in God's image; the following passage has a more male chauvinist view of the same creation:

> Then the LORD God said, "It is not good for man to be alone. I will provide a partner for him." So God formed out of the ground all the wild animals and all the birds of heaven. He brought them to man to see what he would call them, and whatever the man called each living creature, that was its name. Thus the man gave names to all cattle, to the birds of heaven, and to every wild animal; but for the man himself no partner had yet been found. And so the LORD God put the man into a trance, and while he slept, he took one of his ribs and closed the flesh over the place. The LORD God then built up the rib, which he had taken out of the man, into a woman. He brought her to the man, and the man said:
>
> > Now this, at last —
> > bone from my bones,

---

*Copyright ©1962 by the Houghton Mifflin Company. Used by permission.

flesh from my flesh! —
this shall be called woman,
for from man was this taken.

This is why a man leaves his father and mother and is united to his wife, and the two become one flesh.

Choice three—GENESIS 24:48-51, 58-67

This arranged marriage might have little appeal for a modern couple. Unfortunately the most moving and symbolic part of the story is deleted from the official option, probably for the thoughtful purpose of keeping the reading as brief as possible. However, you may want to consider its inclusion for it shows the eagerness of Rebecca to embrace her destiny once it has been made known to her. Her parents, having agreed to the marriage, wish to keep her home a while longer, but Rebecca wants no delay, choosing to set out immediately to greet her unknown bridegroom:

> I blessed the LORD the God of my master Abraham, who had led me by the right road to take my master's niece for his son. Now tell me if you will keep faith and truth with my master. If not, say so, and I will turn elsewhere.
>
> Laban and Bethuel answered, "This is from the Lord; we can say nothing for or against. Here is Rebecca herself; take her, and go. She shall be the wife of your master's son, as the LORD has decreed." They said, "Let us call the girl and see what she says." They called Rebecca and asked her if she would go with the man, and she said, "Yes, I will go." So they let their sister Rebecca and her nurse go with Abraham's servant and his men. They blessed Rebecca and said to her:
>> You are our sister, may you be the mother of myriads; may your sons possess the cities of their enemies.
>
> Then Rebecca and her companions mounted their camels at once and followed the man. So the servant took Rebecca and went his way.
>
> Isaac meanwhile had moved on as far as Beer-lahai-roi and was living in the Negeb. One evening when he had gone out into the open country hoping to meet

49

them, he looked up and saw camels approaching. When Rebecca raised her eyes and saw Isaac, she slipped hastily from her camel, saying to the servant, "Who is that man walking across the open towards us?" The servant answered, "It is my master." So she took her veil and covered herself. The servant related to Isaac all that had happened. Isaac conducted her into the tent and took her as his wife. So she became his wife, and he loved her and was consoled for the death of his mother.

Choice four—TOBIT 7:9c-10, 11c-17 (Vulgate)

Another arranged marriage with an eerie allegorical twist not included in this reading — the seven previous husbands of Sarah had died on their wedding night:

Tobias said to Raphael, "Azarias, my friend, ask Raguel to give me Sarah, my kinswoman." Raguel overheard and said to the young man: "Eat, drink, and be happy tonight. There is no one but yourself who should have my daughter Sarah; indeed I have no right to give her to anyone else, since you are my nearest kinsman. But I must tell you the truth, my son." Tobias answered, "I will not eat or drink anything here until you have disposed of this business of mine." Raguel said to him, "I will do so: I give her to you as the ordinance in the book of Moses prescribes. Heaven has ordained that she shall be yours. Take your kinswoman. From now on, you belong to her and she to you: she is yours forever from this day. The Lord of heaven prosper you both this night, my son, and grant you mercy and peace."

Raguel sent for his daughter Sarah, and when she came he took her hand and gave her to Tobias, saying: "Take her to be your wedded wife in accordance with the law and the ordinance written in the book of Moses. Keep her and take her home to your father; and may the God of heaven keep you safe and give you peace and prosperity." Then he sent for her mother and told her to bring paper, and he wrote out a marriage contract granting Sarah to Tobias as his wife as the law of Moses ordains. After that they began to eat and drink. [Tobit 8c-10, 11c-15 (NEB)]

Choice five—TOBIT 8:4-9

The tragic fate of the other bridegrooms accounts for the fervency of the couple's prayer; still it is a lovely one and kneeling together to ask God's blessing, a sound beginning for a wedding night:

> When they were left alone and the door was shut, Tobias rose from the bed and said to Sarah, "Get up, my love; let us pray and beseech our Lord to show mercy and keep us safe." Tobias said: "We praise thee, O God of our fathers, we praise thy name for ever and ever. Let the heavens and all thy creation praise thee for ever. Thou madest Adam, and Eve his wife to be his helper and support; and those two were the parents of the human race. This was thy word: 'It is not good for man to be alone; let us make him a helper like him.' I now take this my beloved to wife, not out of lust but in true marriage. Grant that she and I may find mercy and grow old together."

Choice six—SONG OF SONGS 2:8-10, 14, 16a; 8:6-7a

This canticle is a sensual, soaring love song that a bride and groom sing in praise of one another's physical beauty and as a pledge of their enduring love. It is most significant if the bride and groom themselves deliver this reading in parts:

Bride: Hark! My beloved! Here he comes,
bounding over the mountains,
leaping over the hills.
   My beloved is like a gazelle
   or a young wild goat:
   there he stands outside our wall,
peeping in at the windows,
glancing through the lattice.

My beloved answered, he said to me:
   Rise up my darling;
   my fairest, come away.

Groom: My dove, that hides in holes in the cliffs
   or in crannies on the high ledges,
let me see your face, let me hear your voice;
for your voice is pleasant, your face is lovely.

Bride: My beloved is mine and I am his.

Groom: Wear me as a seal upon your heart,
            as a seal upon your arm;
            for love is strong as death,
            passion cruel as the grave;
            it blazes up like blazing fire,
            fiercer than any flame.
            Many waters cannot quench love,
            no flood can sweep it away.

Though the official reading is beautifully put together it is possible that other passages appeal to you more. Read the entire *Song of Songs* to discover if this is true for you and work out a passage that satisfies. Read this love song anyway and savor the poetry of the Bible. You might find here ideas for your invitation, program notes, banners, or readings in other parts of the liturgy.

It is also possible to substitute a song in solo or duet for this reading. In the mountains of Vermont a small, vital community of monks create their own attractive music for their liturgy celebrations and among their simple guitar arrangements is the following gentle excerpt from the *Song of Songs:*

Come Now, My Love

Weston Priory
Gregory Norbet, O.S.B.

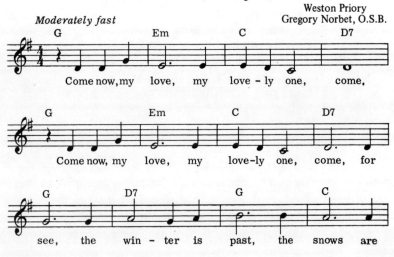

Moderately fast

Come now, my love, my love - ly one, come.

Come now, my love, my love-ly one, come, for

see, the win - ter is past, the snows are

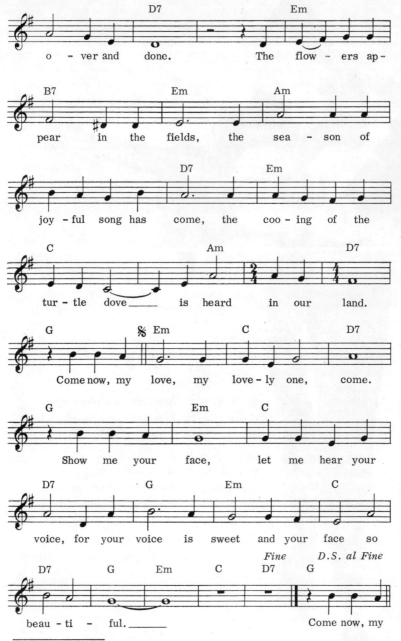

o - ver and done. The flow - ers ap-
pear in the fields, the sea - son of
joy - ful song has come, the coo - ing of the
tur - tle dove____ is heard in our land.
Come now, my love, my love - ly one, come.
Show me your face, let me hear your
voice, for your voice is sweet and your face so
beau - ti - ful._____ Come now, my

* By Gregory Norbet, O.S.B., from the album *Locusts and Wild Honey,* produced by Weston Priory Productions, Weston, Vermont. Used by permission.

53

Come Now, My Love

Come now, my love, my lovely one, come.
Come now, my love, my lovely one, come, for
see, the winter is past, the snows are
over and done. The flowers ap-
pear in the fields, the season of
joyful song has come, the cooing of the
turtle dove — is heard in our land.
Come now, my love, my lovely one, come.
Show me your face, let me hear your
voice, for your voice is sweet and your face so
beautiful. Come now, my

Choice seven—ECCLESIASTICUS 26:1-4, 16-21

In general Ecclesiasticus does not appeal to women's liberationists, but the following passage treads more softly than others:

A good wife makes a happy husband;
she doubles the length of his life.
A staunch wife is her husband's joy;
he will live out his days in peace.
A good wife means a good life;
she is one of the Lord's gifts to those who fear him.
Rich or poor, they are light-hearted,
and always have a smile on their faces.

A wife's charm is the delight of her husband,
and her womanly skill puts flesh on his bones.
A silent wife is a gift from the Lord;
her restraint is more than money can buy.
A modest wife has charm upon charm;
no scales can weigh the worth of her chastity.
As beautiful as the sunrise in the Lord's heaven
is a good wife in a well-ordered home.

[Ecclesiasticus 26:1-4, 13-16 (NEB)]

Choice eight—JEREMIAH 31:31-32a, 33-34a

The covenant which God makes with us, his people, is reflected in the covenant which you make with one another:

The time is coming, says the LORD, when I will make a new covenant with Israel and Judah. It will not be like the covenant I made with their forefathers when I took them by the hand and led them out of Egypt. Although they broke my covenant, I was patient with them, says the LORD. But this is the covenant which I will make with Israel after those days, says the LORD; I will set my law within them and write it on their hearts; I will become their God and they shall be my people. No longer need they teach one another to know the LORD; all of them, high and low alike, shall know me.

After the Old Testament reading, the reader concludes:

This is the Word of the Lord.

All: Thanks be to God.

Responsorial Psalm

In further acclaim to receiving the Word of God, the people respond in joyous psalm, traditional hymn of praise to the Lord. Your commentator, if you have one, or the reader just finished, or another person of your choosing, can lead in this prayer. The official rite provides you with seven choices of psalm readings; many of them are similar. Usually two verses are recited, then all respond, then another two verses and the response, for example:

> Leader: I will bless the LORD continually; his praise shall be always on my lips. In the LORD I will glory; the humble shall hear and be glad.
>
> All: Taste, then, and see that the Lord is good.
>
> Leader: O glorify the LORD with me, and let us exalt his name together. I sought the LORD's help and he answered me; he set me free from all my terrors.
>
> All: Taste, then, and see that the Lord is good.

The approved responsorial psalms in the official rite follow. Read them through in your Bible and select the verses you prefer. In different Bible translations, psalm numbers may vary by one.

> *Choice one*— Psalm 32:12 and 18, 20-21, 22
> ℞. (5b) The earth is full of the goodness of the Lord.
>
> *Choice two*— Psalm 33:2-3, 4-5, 6-7, 8-9.
> ℞. (2a) I will bless the Lord at all times.
> OR (9a) Taste and see the goodness of the Lord.
>
> *Choice three*— Psalm 102:1-2, 8 and 13, 17-18a
> ℞. (8a) The Lord is kind and merciful.
> OR (17) The Lord's kindness is everlasting to those who fear him.
>
> *Choice four*— Psalm 111:1-2, 3-4, 5-7a, 7bc-8, 9
> ℞. (1b) Happy are those who do what the Lord commands. OR Alleluia.

56

Choice five—Psalm 127:1-2, 3, 4-5
℟. (1a) Happy are those who
fear the Lord.
OR (4) See how the Lord
blesses those who fear him.

Choice six—Psalm 144:8-9, 10 and 15, 17-18
℟. (9a) The Lord is compassionate to all
his creatures.

Choice seven—Psalm 148:1-2, 3-4, 9-10, 11-12ab, 12c-14a
℟. (12c) Let all praise the name of the
Lord. *OR* Alleluia.

New Testament Readings

These readings are taken chiefly from the letters of the
apostles to the first Christians advising them how to live this
new found life in Christ. For this second reading you will
want to select the passage which illustrates most graphically
how the two of you hope to find and share and live your new
found life together:

Choice one—ROMANS 8:31b-35, 37-39

This reading invites your trust in the love of God no matter
what trials you are asked to face:

If God is on our side, who is against us? He did not
spare his own Son, but gave him up for us all; and with
this gift how can he fail to lavish upon us all he has to
give? Who will be the accuser of God's chosen ones? It is
God who pronounces acquittal; then who can condemn?
It is Christ — Christ who died, and, more than that, was
raised from the dead — who is at God's right hand, and
indeed pleads our cause. Then what can separate us
from the love of Christ? Can affliction or hardship? Can
persecution, hunger, nakedness, peril, or the sword? —
and yet, in spite of all, overwhelming victory is ours
through him who loved us. For I am convinced that
there is nothing in death or life, in the realm of spirits or
superhuman powers, in the world as it is or the world as
it shall be, in the forces of the universe, in heights or
depths — nothing in all creation that can separate us
from the love of God in Christ Jesus our Lord.

Choice two—ROMANS 12:1-2, 9-18 (longer)
or 1-2, 9-13 (shorter)

This exhortation to the two of you to open your love to others is a popular choice of couples who want their ceremony to celebrate not only the joy they have in loving one another, but also the happy responsibility they share to be of service to their community. It can be done most effectively in parts with various friends and family members calling out to you their challenge to your humanity and Christianity.

One couple accomplished such a dialogue this way: In their program they explained that some members of the community would find a portion of the reading circled and asked if a guest had such a program (given out at random) would he please read his section when the time came. The groom's sister, pre-warned, read the first part of the text:

Therefore my brothers, I implore you by God's mercy to offer your very selves to him: a living sacrifice, dedicated and fit for his acceptance, the worship offered by mind and heart. Adapt yourselves no longer to the pattern of this present world, but let your minds be remade and your whole nature thus transformed. Then you will be able to discern the will of God, and to know what is good, acceptable, and perfect.

Love in all sincerity, loathing evil and clinging to the good. Let love for our brotherhood breed warmth of mutual affection. Give pride of place to one another in esteem.

With unflagging energy, in ardour of spirit, serve the Lord.

Let hope keep you joyful; in trouble stand firm; persist in prayer.

Contribute to the needs of God's people, and practice hospitality.

Verses 14-18

Call down blessings on your persecutors — blessings, not curses.

With the joyful be joyful, and mourn with the mourners.

Care as much about each other as about yourselves. Do not be haughty, but go about with humble folk. Do not keep thinking how wise you are.

Never pay back evil for evil.

Let your aims be such as all men count honourable.

If possible, so far as it lies with you, live at peace with all men.

Choice three—1 CORINTHIANS 6:13c-15a, 17-20

I've never run across a couple who have made this dour selection and hope I never will:

> But he who links himself with Christ is one with him, spiritually. Shun fornication. Every other sin that a man can commit is outside the body; but the fornicator sins against his own body. Do you not know that your body is a shrine of the indwelling Holy Spirit, and the Spirit is God's gift to you? You do not belong to yourselves; you were bought at a price. Then honour God in your body.

Choice four—1 CORINTHIANS 12:31-13:8a

Another popular choice with couples who seek a selfless, outward-reaching love:

> The higher gifts are those you should aim at. And now I speak to you the best way of all. I may speak in tongues of men or of angels, but if I am without love, I am a sounding gong or a clanging cymbal. I may have the gift of prophecy, and know every hidden truth; I may have faith strong enough to move mountains; but if I have no love, I am nothing. I may dole out all I possess, or even give my body to be burnt, but if I have no love, I am none the better.
>
> Love is patient, is kind and envies no one. Love is never boastful, nor conceited, nor rude; never selfish, not quick to take offence. Love keeps no score of wrongs; does not gloat over other men's sins, but delights in the truth. There is nothing love cannot face; there is no limit to its faith, its hope, and its endurance.
>
> Love will never come to an end.

Choice five—EPHESIANS 5:2a, 21-33 (longer)
or 2a, 25-32 (shorter)

This reading used to be the Epistle in the old wedding Mass when the couple had no options. You can appreciate the freedom of choice in the new rite. Because it was read in their mother's wedding and their sister's, some brides feel sentimental about retaining the familiar. Women's libbers might omit, as is provided in the option, verses 21-24, "wives, be subject to your husbands..." If you are using choice seven in the Old Testament readings, "A good wife...," then the shorter version of this reading, the admonition to husbands, makes a good companion piece.

The reading underlines again the fact that your marriage promise is a sign of the faithful covenant Christ makes with his Church: "Live in love as Christ loved you."

Verses 21-24

Be subject to one another out of reverence for Christ. Wives, be subject to your husbands as to the Lord; for the man is the head of the woman, just as Christ also is the head of the church. Christ is, indeed, the Saviour of the body; but just as the church is subject to Christ, so must woman be to their husbands in everything.

Verses 25-32

Husbands, love your wives, as Christ also loved the church and gave himself up for it, to consecrate it, cleansing it by water and word, so that he might present the church to himself all glorious, with no stain or wrinkle or anything of the sort, but holy and without blemish. In the same way men also are bound to love their wives, as they love their own bodies. In loving his wife a man loves himself. For no one ever hated his own body: on the contrary, he provides and cares for it; and that is how Christ treats the church, because it is his body, of which we are living parts. Thus it is that (in the words of Scripture) "a man shall leave his father and mother and shall be joined to his wife, and the two shall become one flesh." It is a great truth that is hidden here. I for my part refer it to Christ and to the church.

Verse 33

But it applies also individually: each of you must love his wife as his very self; and the woman must see to it that she pays her husband all respect.

Choice six—COLOSSIANS 3:12-17

This passage also instructs a Christ-like love toward each other and, together, toward your community. It is something to be read again when arguments arise for the suggestion "Let Christ's peace be arbiter in your hearts" can become a rally point:

Then put on the garments that suit God's chosen people, his own, his beloved: compassion, kindness, humility, gentleness, patience. Be forbearing with one another, and forgiving, where any of you has cause for complaint: you must forgive as the Lord forgave you. To crown all, there must be love, to bind all together and complete the whole. Let Christ's peace be arbiter in your hearts; to this peace you were called as members of a single body. And be filled with gratitude. Let the message of Christ dwell among you in all its richness. Instruct and admonish each other with the utmost wisdom. Sing thankfully in your hearts to God, with psalms and hymns and spiritual songs. Whatever you are doing, whether you speak or act, do everything in the name of the Lord Jesus, giving thanks to God the Father through him.

Choice seven—1 PETER 3:1-9

Again this reading will probably have little appeal to the modern marriage relationship. Few women call their husbands "master" and Ashley Montagu persuasively disputes the myth of woman's "weaker" body:

In the same way you women must accept the authority of your husbands, so that if there are any of them who disbelieve the Gospel they may be won over, without a word being said, by observing the chaste and reverent behaviour of their wives. Your beauty should reside, not in outward adornment — the braiding of the hair, or jewellery, or dress — but in the inmost centre of your being, with its imperishable ornament, a gentle, quiet spirit, which is of high value in the sight of God. Thus it was among God's people in days of old: the women who fixed hopes on him adorned themselves by submission to their husbands. Such was Sarah, who obeyed Abraham and called him "my master." Her children you have now become, if you do good and show no fear.

In the same way, you husbands must conduct your married life with understanding: pay honour to the woman's body, not only because it is weaker, but also because you share together in the grace of God which gives you life. Then your prayers will not be hindered.

To sum up: be one in thought and feeling, all of you; be full of brotherly affection, kindly and humble-minded. Do not repay wrong with wrong, or abuse with abuse; on the contrary, retaliate with blessing, for a blessing is the inheritance to which you yourselves have been called.

Choice eight—1 JOHN 3:18-24

This passage beautifully affirms the supremacy of conscience and is particularly appropriate for a couple whose life-style is sometimes questioned by their families:

My children, love must not be a matter of words or talk; it must be genuine and show itself in action. This is how we may know that we belong to the realm of truth and convince ourselves in his sight that even if our conscience condemns us, God is greater than our conscience and knows all.

Dear friends, if our conscience does not condemn us, then we can approach God with confidence, and obtain from him whatever we ask, because we are keeping his commands and doing what he approves. This is his command: to give his allegiance to his Son Jesus Christ and love one another as he commanded. When we keep his commands we dwell in him and he dwells in us. And this is how we can make sure he dwells within us: we know it from the Spirit he has given us.

62

Choice nine—1 JOHN 4:7-12

A popular choice again stressing the necessary reaching out of love. Your reader might carry a banner, "God is Love":

Dear friends, let us love one another because love is from God. Everyone who loves is a child of God and knows God, but the unloving know nothing of God. For God is love; and his love was disclosed to us in this, that he sent his only Son into the world to bring us life. The love I speak of is not our love for God, but the love he showed to us in sending his Son as the remedy for the defilement of our sins. If God thus loved us, dear friends, we in turn are bound to love one another. Though God has never been seen by man, God himself dwells in us if we love one another; his love is brought to perfection within us.

Choice ten—REVELATION 19:1, 5-9a

Once more the imagery of Christ as bridegroom:

I heard what sounded like the roar of a vast throng in heaven; and they were shouting: "Alleluia! Victory and glory and power belong to our God."

Then a voice came from the throne which said: "Praise our God, all you his servants, you that fear him, both great and small!"

Again I heard what sounded like a vast crowd, like the noise of rushing water and deep roars of thunder, and they cried:

Alleluia! The Lord our God sovereign over all, has entered on his reign! Exult and shout for joy and do him homage, for this wedding-day of the Lamb has come! His bride has made herself ready, and for her dress she has been given fine linen, clean and shining.

(Now the fine linen signifies the righteous deeds of God's people.)

Then the angel said to me, "Write this: 'Happy are those who are invited to the wedding-supper of the Lamb.' "

At the end of the second reading, the reader concludes:

This is the word of the Lord.

All: Thanks be to God.

Alleluia (stand)

In preparation for the Gospel, we welcome the word with an Alleluia verse, sung, recited or in combination. The rite presents you with four choices:

> God is love;
> let us love one another as he
> has loved us.

> If we love one another
> God will live in us in perfect love.

> He who lives in love, lives in God,
> and God in him.

> Everyone who loves is born of God
> and knows him.

All: Alleluia. Alleluia. Alleluia.

Gospel

Celebrant: The Lord be with you.
All: And also with you.
Celebrant: A reading from the holy gospel according to N.
All: Glory to you, Lord.

You may select your Gospel reading or, especially if he knows you well, leave this up to your priest. It might be interesting to you to see what he chooses. The rite gives you ten Gospel choices:

Choice one—MATTHEW 5:1-12

This is the Sermon on the Mount, the Beatitudes, a lovely guide for your life together, particularly appropriate for peace people:

> When he saw the crowds he went up the hill. There he took his seat, and when his disciples had gathered round him he began to address them. And this is the teaching he gave:
> How blest are those who know their need of God;
> the kingdom of Heaven is theirs.
> How blest are the sorrowful;

they shall find consolation.
How blest are those of a gentle spirit;
    they shall have the earth for their possession.
How blest are those who hunger and thirst
to see right prevail;
    they shall be satisfied.
How blest are those who show mercy;
    mercy shall be shown to them.
How blest are those whose hearts are pure;
    they shall see God.
How blest are the peacemakers;
    God shall call them his sons.
How blest are those who have suffered persecution
for the cause of right;
    the kingdom of Heaven is theirs.
How blest you are, when you suffer insults and
persecution and every kind of calumny for my sake.
Accept it with gladness and exultation, for you have a
rich reward in heaven; in the same way they persecuted
the prophets before you.

Choice two—MATTHEW 5:13-16

A lively challenge to the two of you which recognizes your
unique worth and role in Christ's scheme of creating his
kingdom and your duty to find your talents — and flaunt
them:

   You are salt to the world. And if salt becomes
tasteless, how is its saltness to be restored? It is now
good for nothing but to be thrown away and trodden
underfoot.

   You are light for all the world. A town that stands on
a hill cannot be hidden. When a lamp is lit, it is not put
under the meal-tub, but on the lamp-stand, where it
gives light to everyone in the house. And you, like the
lamp, must shed light among your fellows, so that, when
they see the good you do, they may give praise to your
Father in heaven.

Choice three—MATTHEW 7:21, 24-29 (longer)
21, 24-25 (shorter)

Another challenge by Christ for you to demonstrate an
active, effective love:

Not everyone who calls me "Lord, Lord" will enter the kingdom of Heaven, but only those who do the will of my heavenly Father.

What then of the man who hears these words of mine and acts upon them? He is like a man who had the sense to build his house on rock. The rain came down, the floods rose, the wind blew, and beat upon that house; but it did not fall, because its foundations were on rock.

Verses 26-29

But what of the man who hears these words of mine and does not act upon them? He is like a man who was foolish enough to build his house on sand. The rain came down, the floods rose, the wind blew, and beat upon that house; down it fell with a great crash.

When Jesus had finished this discourse the people were astounded at his teaching; unlike their own teachers he taught with a note of authority.

Choice four—MATTHEW 19:3-6

Formerly this was the only Gospel possibility:

Some Pharisees came and tested him by asking, "Is it lawful for a man to divorce his wife on any and every ground?" He asked in return, "Have you never read that the Creator made them from the beginning male and female?"; and he added, "For this reason a man shall leave his father and mother, and be made one with his wife; and the two shall become one flesh. It follows that they are no longer two individuals: they are one flesh. What God has joined together, man must not separate."

Choice five—MATTHEW 22:35-40

Brief and pertinent and a nice balance if your other readings have been lengthy:

"Master, which is the greatest commandment in the Law?" He answered, " 'Love the Lord your God with all your heart, with all your soul, with all your mind.' That is the greatest commandment. It comes first. The second is like it: 'Love your neighbour as yourself.' Everything in the Law and the prophets hangs on these two commandments."

Choice six—MARK 10:6-9

A shorter, less stern version of choice four. This passage might be illustrated by slides of you as children with your parents and now as adults with one another:

In the beginning, at the creation, God made them male and female. For this reason a man shall leave his father and mother, and be made one with his wife; and the two shall become one flesh. It follows that they are no longer two individuals: they are one flesh. What God has joined together, man must not separate.

Choice seven—JOHN 2:1-11

Christ celebrated his first miracle in a happy salute to a wedding feast:

On the third day there was a wedding at Cana-in-Galilee. The mother of Jesus was there, and Jesus and his disciples were guests also. The wine gave out, so Jesus's mother said to him, "They have no wine left." He answered, "Your concern, mother, is not mine. My hour has not yet come." His mother said to the servants, "Do whatever he tells you." There were six stone water-jars standing near, of the kind used for Jewish rites of purification; each held from twenty to thirty gallons. Jesus said to the servants, "Fill the jars with water," and they filled them to the brim. "Now draw some off," he ordered, "and take it to the steward of the feast"; and they did so. The steward tasted the water now turned into wine, not knowing its source; though the servants who had drawn the water knew. He hailed the bridegroom and said, "Everyone serves the best wine first, and waits until the guests have drunk freely before serving the poorer sort; but you have kept the best wine till now."

This deed at Cana-in-Galilee is the first of the signs by which Jesus revealed his glory and led his disciples to believe in him.

Choice eight—JOHN 15:9-12

Another beautiful commandment to love:

As the Father has loved me, so I have loved you. Dwell in my love. If you heed my commands, you will dwell in my love, as I have heeded my Father's commands and dwell in his love.

I have spoken thus to you, so that my love may be in you, and your love complete. This is my commandment: love one another, as I have loved you.

Choice nine—JOHN 15:12-16

Again an exhortation for you to share together in Christ's ministry of love and service, perhaps more outward looking than the reading above:

This is my commandment: love one another, as I have loved you. There is no greater love than this, that a man should lay down his life for his friends. You are my friends, if you do what I command you. I call you servants no longer; a servant does not know what his master is about. I have called you friends, because I have disclosed to you everything that I heard from my Father. You did not choose me: I chose you. I appointed you to go on and bear fruit, fruit that shall last; so that the Father may give you all that you ask in my name.

Choice ten—JOHN 17:20-26 (longer) 20-23 (shorter)

The prayer of Christ in which he asks his Father to recognize your partnership with the Son:

But it is not for these alone that I pray, but for those also who through their words put their faith in me; may they all be one: as thou, Father, art in me, and I in thee, so also may they be in us, that the world may believe that thou didst send me. The glory which thou gavest me I have given to them, that they may be one, as we are one; I in them and thou in me, may they be perfectly one. Then the world will learn that thou didst send me, that thou didst love them as thou didst me.

Verses 24-26

Father, I desire that these men, who are thy gift to me, may be with me where I am, so that they may look upon my glory, which thou hast given me because thou didst love me before the world began. O righteous Father, although the world does not know thee, I know thee, and these men know that thou didst send me. I made thy name known to them, and will make it known, so that the love thou hadst for me may be in them, and I may be in them.

After the Gospel, the priest concludes:

This is the gospel of the Lord.

All: Praise to you, Lord Jesus Christ.

The Homily

The official rite suggests that the priest "speaks about the mystery of Christian marriage, the dignity of wedded love, the grace of the sacrament and the responsibilities of married people, keeping in mind the circumstances of this particular marriage."

The better your priest or minister who is delivering the homily knows you, the more he can make this part of the ceremony custom-fit your marriage. The homily is an important, relaxed and personal moment of communication and your priest will welcome any ideas you have toward making his brief remarks appropriate and alive.

A meaningful homily will long remain with you and your friends. Here are a few ideas, to spark your own imagination, which couples and guests have remembered thoughtfully and gratefully from other wedding celebrations:

. . . Grant and Gigi this afternoon accept one another with all the confidence and commitment and enthusiasm in the world and they have invited all of you here to witness their marriage contract, this ultimate outward sign which reveals the maturity and conviction of their inward feelings. They have invited you to their wedding because you are all people from whom Grant and Gigi learn, people Grant and Gigi care about, people Grant and Gigi in some way count on, look up to, enjoy. When Grant and Gigi make their pledge to one another, you must make to yourself, your pledge to them: "If ever they need me I will be there."

But right now it is much more true that we need Grant and Gigi. Today we draw from the freshness and anticipation of their love, the revitalization of our own. When Grant and Gigi make their promise to each other, those of you who are married can remember how you felt on your own wedding day when your faith in each other was so full, so capable of every challenge, and you can renew your vows and reaffirm your faith. Those of us who are not married can contemplate a mystery and pay tribute to this example of love and trust, a sign of the fidelity of Christ's love for us all. We are all in a way married, for to be really alive every one of us must make our active commitment to something.

. . . Your love is never static. It grows or it withdraws. Let Bob Dylan's lyrics urge you to work at it. You can't stand still on a steep mountain climb, you either move up or slide down, ". . . people who are not busy being born are busy dying. . . "

. . . Excerpts from the old and familiar Exhortation Before Marriage are still requested by some brides because it is a link with past weddings which have meaning to them. Aside from its traditional value, it is beautifully written and complete:

As you know, you are about to enter into a union which is most sacred and most serious, a union which was established by God himself. . . Because God himself is thus its author, marriage is of its very nature a holy institution, requiring of those who enter into it a complete and unreserved giving of self. But Christ our Lord added to the holiness of marriage an even deeper meaning and a higher beauty. He referred to the love of marriage to describe his own love for his Church, that is, for the people of God whom he redeemed by his own blood. . .

This union then is most serious, because it will bind you together for life in a relationship so close and so intimate that it will profoundly influence your whole future. That future, with its hopes and disappointments, its successes and its failures, its pleasures and its pains, its joys and its sorrows, is hidden from your eyes. You know that these elements are mingled in every life and are to be expected in your own. And so, not knowing what is before you, you take each other for better or for worse, for richer or for poorer, in sickness and in health, until death.

70

Truly, then, these words are most serious. It is a beautiful tribute to your undoubted faith in each other, that, recognizing their full import, you are nevertheless so willing and ready to pronounce them. And because these words involve such solemn obligations, it is most fitting that you rest the security of your wedded life upon the great principle of self-sacrifice. And so you begin your married life by the voluntary and complete surrender of your individual lives in the interest of that deeper and wider life which you are to have in common. Henceforth you belong entirely to each other; you will be one in mind, one in heart and one in affections. And whatever sacrifices you may hereafter be required to make to preserve this common life, always make them generously. Sacrifice is usually difficult and irksome. Only love can make it easy; and perfect love can make it a joy.

... One celebrant played his talk around a portion of the old exhortation above, "... That future with its hopes and disappointments, its successes and its failures, its pleasures and its pains. ... " and asked the question Nietzsche asked in *Thus Spake Zarathustra,* "Have you ever said Yes to a single joy? O my friends, then you said Yes too to all woe." The homilist emphasized the frequent fun of Yes, the sometimes sorrow of Yes, but above all the constant Yes of love.

You may wish, instead of a monologue, a dialogue homily, giving your family and friends the chance to say a few words to you. If you decide this, unless you've assembled an unusually uninhibited and loquacious group, it is probably best to set up a few plants in the congregation who'll respond immediately to the invitation to contribute. If your ceremony thus far has succeeded in creating a joyful atmosphere of sharing and participation and your guests are encouraged by the first speakers, then the dialogue should come off comfortably, particularly if the group is small and the liturgical space open. In a large crowd or where church pillars hide and make inaudible anyone rising from among the congregation, the dialogue homily is best omitted.

This is the first part of the Liturgy of the Word. Now it is time for your words to each other.

THE EXCHANGE OF VOWS AND RINGS

This is the moment not to be missed. It is why you two are here, why the celebration, why all these people have come together. You are about to make your marriage promise to each other. Stop the action! Frame it! Shout it! In every way possible what you are about to do must be announced, called attention to, spotlighted. This is it!

Setting the Scene

It has been traditional for all to rise when the time comes for the bride and groom to exchange their vows. However, depending on the physical makeup of their church and the number of friends gathered, some couples have found it easier for guests to hear and see when they remain seated. The bride and groom should step up to the highest point of the sanctuary, facing the congregation either full-face or semi-side face, if this is more comfortable.

The priest, instead of standing over them, should remove himself as far as is practical from center stage so that everyone appreciates the wonderful fact that the two of you are the ministers of this sacrament. One sensitive pastor suggests to a couple that they move to the center in front of

God, let me be <u>conscious</u> of it! Let me
be <u>conscious</u> of what is happening <u>while</u> it
is happening. Let me realize it and feel it
vividly. Let not the consciousness of this
event (as happens so often) come to me
tardily, so that I half miss the experience.
Let me be <u>conscious</u> of it!
                    —*Anne Morrow Lindbergh*

the altar table while he places himself a step lower and to the
side and invites the official witnesses to stand with him.

You may elect a song like "There Is Love" as an
introduction to your marriage rite or herald the event with a
trumpet blast. At this point, one couple sent children among
the guests to distribute roll-up pipe noisemakers with
instructions to blow after the vows were exchanged. Another
couple had the procession of the two small ringbearers, a boy
and a girl, a delightful and charming pause in the ceremony
which highlighted marvelously what was to come.

Generally your priest alerts everyone to the occasion
with a few warm and slowly spoken words and the invitation
to you to declare your marriage intention.

The official rite provides the priest with an introduction
but also tells him he might address the couple in other similar
words. It may be as simple as:

Maureen, will you tell us if you will be married with
Tom?
Tom, will you tell us if you will be married with
Maureen?

Or, the celebrant might call attention to the moment by
reminding all of the special role you wish them to play as

witnesses of your promise:

Friends, Anne and Brian are about to marry one another. This is the most important moment of today for them and for you because, as you know, you are here not as audience, but as witnesses of a new life together about to begin. Anne and Brian don't want you to miss their vows and they invite you to stay seated so that you will be better able to share this moment with them...

The priest then turned to the couple and spoke to them in the words suggested by the rite:

My dear friends, you have come together in this church so that the Lord may seal and strengthen your love in the presence of the Church's minister and this community. Christ abundantly blesses this love. He has already consecrated you in baptism and now he enriches and strengthens you by a special sacrament so that you may assume the duties of marriage in mutual and lasting fidelity. And so, in the presence of the Church, I ask you to state your intentions.

Although the official rite provides three probing questions about freedom of choice, intent of fidelity, and the raising of children, to be asked by the priest and answered by you prior to your exchange of vows, the introduction to the rite most thoughtfully provides: "If it seems more suitable, even the questions before the consent may be omitted as long as the priest asks and receives the consent of the contracting parties." Happily most priests and couples agree to dispense with these self-evident questions, and immediately following the invitation of the priest, the couple face each other, joining their right hands or both hands or whatever pleases them. They then make their vows to one another, speaking from memory or reading from a card which each holds, but certainly not in the old "repeat after me" fashion. The groom usually speaks first, but you may make your own decision.

Speaking Your Vows

In the United States the rite provides a choice between two forms of the marriage consent:

I, N., take you, N., to be my wife (husband). I promise to be

74

true to you in good times and in bad, in sickness and in health. I will love you and honor you all the days of my life.

I, N., take you, N., for my lawful wife (husband), to have and to hold, from this day forward, for better, for worse, for richer, for poorer, in sickness and in health, until death do us part.

Note that neither the old consent nor the two of the new rite contain the word "obey."

In many churches, hopefully in yours, you will not have to use these formulas, lovely as they are, but will be encouraged to compose your own vows. It is not an easy thing to actually sit down and write a vow which expresses what you really want to say about your feelings for one another and the sacrament you share. But it is a good thing to try and do it. Even if you must use an official contract, or fall back on one because you can't get the pen to write, challenge yourself with a few attempts to put your thoughts in writing.

Perhaps the funniest yet most serious wee morning hours we ever spent were with a couple the early a.m. before their wedding. They had cheerfully promised their priest their vows a few days before their wedding, then had promised to provide them "at the rehearsal"; now they were hoping to make the ceremony. The bride had in mind a confessional type of vow and a life-style agreement. The groom had in mind saying "I do," but was successfully persuaded otherwise. The idea was for their friends to tell them all their faults and in their vows they would promise to try and correct them. We obliged with a litany of imperfections, most of which they rejected, and the discussion began to descend to the subject of the future bride's cooking which we earnestly hoped would improve. Amidst the banter, however, certain tendencies toward stubbornness, nagging and unreality were admitted.

When we left, the couple had composed a long dialogue vow that alternated between breast-beating and extravagant promises with specific concessions to women's lib.

What we heard the next day was a very simple four line promise, quite similar to that of the official rite, in which each vowed, "to cherish and honor you as you are, to help

75

you be all you can be." As literature it was neither an especially eloquent nor original piece of writing, but those of us who had witnessed the behind-the-scenes hilarity and thoughtfulness knew how much it said, and the bride and groom knew exactly what it meant.

There seem to be two schools of thought among couples who compose their own vows. One is that they are two distinct individuals with different gifts and different needs and their promises to each other should, therefore, be different:

Helen, before our friends I ask to be your husband, your companion in life. I promise you respect, freedom, encouragement and all help necessary to develop yourself fully as the person you are. Will you be patient and love me as we learn together?

I give you this ring as a sign of our love and a symbol of the sacrament we make with each other. + God.

Ray, before our friends I ask to be your wife, your companion in life. I promise you patience and support in the finding and development of your goals and respect for the decisions they will cause you to make. Will you be understanding and love me as we learn together?

I give you this ring as a sign of our love and a symbol of the sacrament we make with each other. + God.

Other couples feel that, since they are entering a life where two shall be one, their vows to one another should be the same:

Nancy, in the presence of this community, I ask you to be my wife.

I am and will always be your wife, John. In the presence of this community, I ask you to be my husband.

I am and always will be your husband. I join you, Nancy, for love, for life; to live and grow in the beauty of our nearness; to be with you now and always; to stand by you and move with you through whatever our married life may bring; to ever and everywhere be your husband.

I join you, John, for love, for life; to live and grow in

and the nearness of God

the beauty of our nearness; to be with you now and always; to stand by you and move with you through whatever our married life may bring; to ever and everywhere be your wife.

Acknowledgment of Vows

After the couple have exchanged their vows, the Church acknowledges their marriage by receiving their consent. The rite provides the priest with these words:

You have declared your consent before the Church. May the Lord in his goodness strengthen your consent and fill you both with his blessings.
What God has joined, men must not divide.
℟. Amen.

You and your priest, however, may opt for a more obvious affirmation of the great event which has just taken place. The celebrant may reach for your hands or embrace you and announce to your guests:

I say, with all who are here, that we have witnessed the sacrament which you have made together. You are husband and wife. Let us celebrate this wedding!

And then, immediately, a spontaneous joyful reaction. Depending on your personal style, your guests might burst into applause, or blow their noisemakers, or release balloons. They might sing together briefly a song they all know such as "What The World Needs Now Is Love" or the first verse of the more staid, "Now Thank We All our God," or hear from the magnificent organ a quick hallelujah from Handel's "Hallelujah Chorus." You might kiss each other and receive congratulations from family and friends who come forward. Or, no noise; after the acknowledgment by the priest and at his invitation your guests may recite together an affirmation which you have included in their program: "Anne and Brian, we have seen and heard you pledge your sacred commitment to each other and greeting you as husband and wife, we offer you our love and support."

After all have testified that a marriage has taken place, the priest might present the official witnesses with the marriage certificate which they sign, in obvious gesture, as a symbol to all. These two, if they are a married couple, or another couple of your designation may step forward and say: "We welcome you to the community of married people whom God calls to be forever a witness of his love and a service to his people." One couple then offered a prayer for the newlyweds:

Ever since the day we heard of it, we have not ceased to pray for you. We ask God that you may receive from him all wisdom and spiritual understanding for full insight into his will, so that your manner of life may be worthy of the Lord and entirely pleasing to him. We pray that you may bear fruit in active goodness of every kind, and grow in the knowledge of God. May he strengthen you, in his glorious might, with ample power to meet whatever comes with fortitude, patience and joy; and give thanks to the Father who has made you fit to share the heritage of God's people in the realm of light. *[Colossians 1:9-12]*

Blessing and Exchanging Rings

In the official rite the blessing and exchange of rings come after the exchange of vows and the Church's reception of your consent. However, many couples have sensibly chosen to make the exchange of rings a part of their vows to one another, as in one of the examples above, thereby linking the visible symbol of fidelity instantly to the promise. The rite provides the priest with three different blessings for the rings and suggests words that the couple might use in placing the ring on one another's fingers:

Choice one

May the Lord bless † these rings
which you give to each other
as the sign of your love and fidelity.
 ℟. **Amen.**

Choice two

Lord, bless these rings which we bless †
in your name.
Grant that those who wear them
may always have a deep faith in each other.

78

May they do your will
and always live together
in peace, good will and love.
We ask this through Christ our Lord.

    ℞. Amen.

Choice three

Lord,
bless and consecrate N. and N.
in their love for each other.
May these rings be a symbol
of true faith in each other,
and always remind them of their love.
(We ask this) through Christ our Lord.

    ℞. Amen.

As they exchange rings the bride and groom may say to each other:

N., take this ring as a sign of my love and fidelity. In the name of the Father, and of the Son, and of the Holy Spirit.

When the rings are given as part of the marriage vow, you may decide to have the priest bless the rings before your exchange of vows, immediately following his invitation to you to declare your consent. Or — and this probably works more smoothly — after the vows and rings have been exchanged and the priest and your guests have affirmed your marriage, he might take both your ringed hands in his and bless the rings.

As your vows to each other are the visible, outward sign of your marriage sacrament and should, therefore, be set apart and made obvious in every way possible so that you and your guests will be deeply conscious of this mystery, so, too, do the rings have particular symbolic value in your wedding ritual. Since ancient times the circle of a ring has signified eternal love and everlasting faithfulness. The exchange should be slow and deliberate, capable of being seen by everyone. As Rev. Joseph M. Champlin suggests in his book, *Together For Life,* a good way to exchange rings is to have one partner place the ring halfway on the other's finger symbolizing an offering of self and desire of acceptance. The other partner then slides the ring down to its proper place symbolizing "yes."

Before he gave his bride the ring, one groom recited a poem suggesting its meaning:

Love Song

This, that I carry like a butterfly,
prisoner in my cupped and outstretched hands,
is, of all things, small,
but great in its demands
and bears within itself a world of power.
I close my hand upon it like a wall.
For this there can be neither time nor season
and of all things upon the earth
it has the least to do with reason.
(I open my hand, finger from palm. Look!)
This holds within it life, death, and birth;
used wrong, there is no harm it cannot do.
Look long, look carefully;
this is for you.*

He then gave the ring to his bride saying: "Take and wear this ring as a sign of our love."

In recent years in the United States the overwhelming number of bridegrooms do decide to have a double-ring ceremony, thereby opposing a double standard of the bride as "claimed" and the groom as "free." Even when they don't intend to wear it, men have recognized the genuine symbolism of the ring and have wanted to receive one during the ceremony. One practical-minded couple, when the groom made known his agreement with the sentiments of ring ceremony but his reluctance to wear one, decided to substitute a key ring which he would use every day to enter their home. This would be his "wedding ring." They didn't announce the substitution to their guests, but the bride simply put this in his hand at the appropriate time during the ceremony.

---

* By John R. Nash, from *Poetry U.S.A.*, ed. by Paul Molloy, © 1968, Scholastic Book Services.

Making Personal Statements

When the vows and rings have been exchanged and recognized, many couples find this a most significant time to make their personal statement about marriage. This might take the form of a self-composed dialogue prayer, a Bible or secular reading, a poem, a song lyric, a declaration of the decisions you have made together about your life-style, anything that says specifically what you want yourself and each other and your friends to understand about your commitment. Probably you need no ideas to stimulate your creativity here. Undoubtedly there is some reading or song or personal philosophy discovered early in your love together or which you brought with you to that love, that you have used as a reference point throughout your engagement. This is your prayer. However, in the Appendix and below are a few readings which other couples, with whom you have, at least, recent marriage in common, have thought pertinent to their situation. You might enjoy sharing their feelings with them.

Recited by a bride:

About Marriage

Don't lock me in wedlock, I want
marriage, an
encounter-

I told you about the
green light of
May

    (a veil of quiet befallen
    the downtown park,
    late

    Saturday after
    noon, long
    shadows and cool

    air, scent of
    new grass,
    fresh leaves,

    blossom on the threshold of
    abundance-

    and the birds I met there,

birds of passage breaking their journey,
three birds each of a different species:

the azalea-breasted with round poll, dark,
the brindled, merry, mousegliding one,
and the smallest, golden as gorse and wearing
a black Venetian mask

and with them the three douce hen-birds
feathered in tender, lively brown-

I stood
a half-hour under the enchantment,
no-one passed near,
the birds saw me and

let me be near them.)
It's not
irrelevant:
I would be
met

and meet you
so,
in a green

airy space, not
locked in.*

One couple took their inspiration from the letters of Eldridge Cleaver and Beverly Axelrod:

Groom: " . . . . I feel humiliated by the words you inspire me to write to you. I refuse to write them. What right have you to summon my soul from its slumber? But it's all golden and I write this from a sense of the sweetness of irony. . . . You have tossed me a life-line. . . . since encountering you, I feel life strength. . . . My step, the tread of my stride, which was becoming tentative and uncertain, has begun to recover and take on new definiteness, a confidence, a boldness which makes me want to kick over a few tables. I may even swagger a little, and, as I read in a book somewhere, 'push myself forward like a train.' "

* By Denise Levertov, from O *Taste and See.* Copyright © 1963 by Denise Levertov Goodman. "About Marriage" was first published in *Poetry.* Reprinted by permission of New Directions Publishing Corporation.

Bride: "Believe this: I accept you. I know you little and I know you much, but whichever way it goes, I accept you. Your manhood comes through in a thousand ways, rare and wonderful. I'm out in the world with an infinity of choices. You don't have to wonder if I'm grasping at something because I have no real measuring stick. I accept you. . . . What an awesome thing it is to feel oneself on the verge of the possibility of really knowing another person. Can it ever happen? I'm not sure. I don't know that any two people can really strip themselves that naked in front of each other. . . . Of all the dangers we share, probably the greatest comes from our fantasizing about each other. Are we making each other up?. . . "

Groom: "Your thought, 'Of all the dangers we share, probably the greatest comes from our fantasizing about each other. Are we making each other up?' bothers me. It would be very simple if that were the case. . . . But it is not that easy, is it? I seek a lasting relationship, something permanent in a world of change. . . . The reason two people are reluctant to really strip themselves naked in front of each other is because in doing so they make themselves vulnerable and give enormous power over themselves one to the other. . . . How often, indeed, they end by inflicting pain and torment upon each other. Better to maintain shallow, superficial affairs; that way the scars are not too deep, no blood is hacked from the soul. . . . Getting to know someone, entering that new world, is an ultimate, irretrievable leap into the unknown. . . . I know that sometimes people fake on each other out of genuine motives to hold onto the object of their tenderest feelings. They see themselves as so inadequate that they feel forced to wear a mask in order to continuously impress the other. I do not want to "hold" you, I want you to "stay" out of your own need for me. . . . We recognize each other. And, having recognized each other, is it any wonder that our souls hold hands and cling together even while our minds equivocate, hesitate, vacillate, and tremble?" *

Together a couple recited Psalm 67 (NEB):

> God be gracious to us and bless us,
> God make his face shine upon us,
> that his ways may be known on earth
> and his saving power among all the nations.
> Let the peoples praise thee, O God;
> Let all peoples praise thee.
> Let all nations rejoice and shout in triumph;
> for thou dost judge the peoples with justice
> and guidest the nations of the earth.
> Let the peoples praise thee, O God;
> let all peoples praise thee.
> The earth has given its increase
> and God, our God will bless us . . . .

Another chose Leviticus:

> If you conform to my statutes, if you observe my commandments and carry them out, I will give you rain at the proper time; the land shall yield its produce and the trees of the country-side their fruit. Threshing shall last till vintage and vintage till sowing; you shall eat your fill and live secure in your land. I will give peace in the land, and you shall lie down to sleep with no one to terrify you. I will rid your land of dangerous beasts and it shall not be ravaged by war. . . . I will look upon you with favour, I will make you fruitful and increase your numbers: I will give my covenant with you its full effect. Your old harvest shall last you in store until you have to clear out the old to make room for the new. I will establish my Tabernacle among you and will not spurn you. I will walk to and fro among you; I will become your God and you shall become my people.
>
> *[Leviticus 26:2-7, 9-12]*

And another wrote their own prayer:

> Dear God, together we begin our prayer to you, that you will bless the promises we have just made to each other and show us how it is that together we might love and serve you and be to ourselves, our friends and family a witness of your love, a support in time of need, and a joy always.

Groom: Dear God, the world I knew as a single man was not a good one and I have done very little to seek new methods of confronting its ills. You have given me a wife in whom I see great goodness; I pray that I don't selfishly enjoy this goodness only in my own home and among our friends, but encourage it to extend outward toward our larger community. And I pray that Maureen's goodness will inspire me to grow in caring and concern so that the two of us will work together toward making our world a healthy, happy place for our children and all children.

Bride: Friend Jesus, the role of a wife and mother appeals to me and I pray that you help me be a source of serenity and strength in our home, a pleasure and a help to Tom, a good example and fun for our children. But I also pray that I do not hide in our house away from all the problems of the world and away from the talents you have given me. Give me the energy to seek challenges for myself and together with my husband to recognize our responsibility toward trying to effect your design for the world.

General Intercessions

The Liturgy of the Word and your marriage rite end with the Universal Prayer or Prayer of the Faithful, a most fitting finale and summation, for this is the prayer of everyone present and it is a prayer which any and all have the privilege of creating. Although there is a certain structure to the Prayer of the Faithful, there is no strict formula for its content. You and your guests are invited to express your prayer for the needs of one another, the Church, the country, the world. It is a particularly apt time to pray for the private love of the couple for one another and for the bride and groom to pray for parents and family and demonstrate the social concerns of their conscience. One leader might plead each intercession, or the bride and groom may each offer a prayer, and their parents and friends might speak out with prepared requests. There might also be a time at the end for anyone among the guests to rise spontaneously and petition and for all to make their silent prayer. The example below borrows from the intercessions of several wedding ceremonies:

Celebrant: For ourselves, for all the human family, and especially for this husband and this wife, let us appeal to God.

Groom: For my wife, that I will love her as she deserves and love her more tomorrow, we pray to the Lord.

All: Lord, hear our prayer.

Bride: For my husband, that I will love him now and always and that we may grow old together, we pray to the Lord.

All: Lord, hear our prayer.

Couple: For our parents, that they may reap a harvest of even deeper joys from the seeds they have so lovingly sown, we pray to the Lord.

All: Lord, hear our prayer.

Father of the Bride: For our children, that we might learn love from them and know when to step in and when to step out of their lives, we pray to the Lord.

All: Lord, hear our prayer.

Mother of the Groom: For the children of our children, if they should be blessed with them, that from harmony and love in parents they may draw the sustenance of happy and productive lives and that they may give to their parents the great joy which our children have given us, we pray to the Lord.

All: Lord, hear our prayer.

Leader: For a world to live in where the air is clean, the water pure, the people at peace and justice prevails, we pray to the Lord.

All: Lord, hear our prayer.

Leader: For all couples who are married today, sharing from now on a wedding anniversary with Grant and Gigi, we pray to the Lord.

All: Lord, hear our prayer.

Leader: For the community of all of us here, that we will celebrate this marriage with great gladness, we pray to the Lord.

All: Lord, hear our prayer.

When the prepared petitions are over, your priest or commentator might invite your guests' contributions: "Do you have a special wish for Grant and Gigi? Say it now!"

After all the petitions have been made, the priest draws what has been said into a brief final prayer which applies not only to the nuptial couple, but to all the church. He concludes:

. . . through Christ our Lord.

All: Amen.

THE LITURGY OF THE EUCHARIST

Your wedding Mass resumes with the offertory, the preparation of gifts. It is most fitting and symbolic that the first
thing the two of you do together as man and wife is to
lovingly prepare the Lord's banquet table with bread and
wine to nourish your guests, for your marriage is a sign of the
flesh and blood covenant, the nourishment which the risen
Christ has prepared for his people.

Presentation Procession and Song

This part of the Mass offers you enormous possibility of
expressing yourselves your way. Together you may go to the
rear of the church bringing forward bread baked by yourselves or friends, and wine, perhaps made by you or given to
you as a gift. Or others may bring the gifts to you in the
sanctuary where you take them and present them to the
priest. Any family members or close friends whom you want
very much to give a meaningful role in your ceremony can be

When we bless 'the cup of blessing', is it
not a means of sharing in the blood of
Christ? When we break the bread, is it not
a means of sharing in the body of Christ?
Because there is one loaf, we, many as we
are, are one body; for it is one loaf of
which we all partake. — *1 Corinthians 10*

Then you shall be called by a new name
which the LORD shall pronounce with his own lips;
you will be a glorious crown in the LORD's hand,
. . . for the LORD delights in you
    and to him your land is wedded.
    For, as a young man weds a maiden,
    so you shall wed him who rebuilds you,
and your God shall rejoice over you
    as a bridegroom rejoices over the bride.
                 — *Isaiah 62*

asked to take this part. The procession might include more
than the offerings of bread and wine; now might be the time
that you will dress a bare altar table with cloth and
eucharistic necessities and flowers, assisting the priest to
prepare for the sacrament. One couple, having asked each of
their friends to bring a small Christmas gift for the Indian
children in the school where they met, collected these
brightly wrapped packages at the church door. They were
brought up during the presentation and placed against the
side wall of the sanctuary.

Another couple had at this time a "blessing of flowers"
on the altar and then brought to their mothers, until that
moment unadorned, their corsages. Although the couple's
music selections were rock, the offertory song was a maternal
preference, "Ave Maria."

While the offertory procession is taking place, a song
should be sung. It may be a contemporary solo like George
Harrison's:

Within You, Without You

We were talking—about the space between us all
And the people—who hide themselves
behind a wall of illusion
Never glimpse the truth—then it's far too late—
when they pass away.
We were talking—about the love we all
could share—when we find it
To try our best to hold it there—with our love
With our love—we could save the world
—if they only knew.
Try to realize it's all within yourself
no one else can make you change
And to see you're really only very small,
and life flows on within you and without you.
We were talking—about the love that's
gone so cold and the people
who gain the world and lose their soul—
they don't know—they can't see—are you one of them?
When you've seen beyond yourself—
then you may find, peace of mind, is waiting there—
And the time will come when you see
We're all one, and life flows on within you and without
you.*

Or, a small group rendition of "All Good Gifts" from
Godspell with the community singing the refrain:

All Good Gifts

We plow the fields and scatter
The good seed on the land
But it is fed and watered
By God's almighty hand
He sends the snow in winter
The warmth to swell the grain
The breezes and the sunshine
And soft refreshing rain.

All good gifts around us

Are sent from heaven above
Then thank the Lord
O, thank the Lord
For all His love.

We thank Thee then, O Father
For all things bright and good
The seedtime and the harvest
Our life, our health, our food
No gifts have we to offer
For all Thy love imparts
But that which Thou desirest
Our humble, thankful hearts.

All good gifts around us
Are sent from heaven above
Then thank the Lord,
O, thank the Lord
For all His love.*

Or, all might sing together a song which most know such as Ray Repp's "Of My Hands," or Joe Wise's "Take Our Bread."

At their offertory one couple chose to make a most unique gift to one another:

Celebrant: Mary and Bob, do you have any special offering to bring?

Bride: I offer you my name,
Symbol of the life I bring to you.

Groom: I offer you my name,
Symbol of the life I bring to you.

Bride: Will you accept my name,
and hereafter be known as Robert Connelly-Brown.

Groom: Will you accept my name,
and hereafter be known as Mary Connelly-Brown.

Undoubtedly it helps when the names are euphonious.

Invitation to Pray

---

* Lyrics of "All Good Gifts," by Stephen Schwartz, from the production *Godspell*, copyright © 1971 by Valando Music, Inc. (A Metromedia Co.) and New Cadenza Music Corp., 1700 Broadway, New York, N.Y. 10019. Used by permission only. All rights reserved.

Celebrant: Pray, brethren, that our sacrifice may be
acceptable to God, the almighty Father.

All: May the Lord accept the sacrifice at your hands
for the praise and glory of his name,
for our good, and the good of all his Church.

Prayer Over the Gifts

The rite provides you a choice among three simple and appropriate prayers which ask God to accept the gifts offered in your name:

Choice one

Lord,
accept our offering
for this newly-married couple, N. and N.
By your love and providence you have brought
them together;
now bless them all the days of their married life.

Choice two

Lord,
accept the gifts we offer you
on this happy day.
In your fatherly love
watch over and protect N. and N.
whom you have united in marriage.

Choice three

Lord,
hear our prayers
and accept the gifts we offer for N. and N.
Today you have made them one in the sacrament
of marriage.
May the mystery of Christ's unselfish love,
which we celebrate in this eucharist,
increase their love for you and for each other.

Celebrant: (We ask this) through Christ our Lord.
All: Amen.

The Eucharistic Prayer

This is the heart of the Mass, a prayer first of delightful praise and thanksgiving for the Father's gifts, then of remembrance of the Son's life and death and life again, and finally of petition for each to participate with Christ in satisfying the needs of mankind.

Celebrant: The Lord be with you.

     All: And also with you.
Celebrant: Lift up your hearts.
     All: We lift them up to the Lord.
Celebrant: Let us give thanks to the Lord, our God.
     All: It is right to give Him thanks and praise.

The rite authorizes a choice among three prefaces which were designed to emphasize that this Mass is a wedding Mass. Although the prefaces are similar, each has a different rhythm and probably one has particular appeal for you. You might personalize "husband" and "wife" with your names:

Choice one

Father, all-powerful and ever-living God,
we do well always and everywhere to give you thanks.
By this sacrament your grace unites man and woman
in an unbreakable bond of love and peace.

You have designed the chaste love of husband and wife
for the increase both of the human family
and of your own family born in baptism.

You are the loving Father of the world of nature;
you are the loving Father of the new creation of grace.
In Christian marriage you bring together
    the two orders of creation:
nature's gift of children enriches the world
and your grace enriches also your Church.

Through Christ the choirs of angels
and all the saints
praise and worship your glory.
May our voices blend with theirs
as we join in their unending hymn:

Choice two

Father, all powerful and ever-living God,

we do well always and everywhere to give you thanks
through Jesus Christ our Lord.

Through him you entered into a new covenant
    with your people.
You restored man to grace in the
    saving mystery of redemption.
You gave him a share in the divine life
through his union with Christ.
You made him an heir of Christ's eternal glory.

This outpouring of love in the new covenant of grace
is symbolized in the marriage covenant
that seals the love of husband and wife
and reflects your divine plan of love.

And so, with the angels and all the saints in heaven
we proclaim your glory
and join in their unending hymn of praise:

Choice three

Father, all-powerful and ever-living God,
we do well always and everywhere to give you thanks.

You created man in love to share your divine life.
We see this high destiny in the love of husband and wife,
which bears the imprint of your own divine love.

Love is man's origin,
love is his constant calling,
love is his fulfillment in heaven.

The love of man and woman
is made holy in the sacrament of marriage,
and becomes the mirror of your everlasting love.

Through Christ the choirs of angels
and all the saints
praise and worship your glory.
May our voices blend with theirs
as we join in their unending hymn:

All: Holy, holy, holy Lord, God of power and might,
heaven and earth are full of your glory.
Hosanna in the highest.
Blessed is he who comes in the name of the Lord.
Hosanna in the highest.

Of course, the sanctus, above, might also be sung.

The Eucharistic Prayer continues, and it is your choice among the four options contained in the new Order of the Mass and found in your Sunday Mass booklet; none has been specifically written for a wedding. The marriage rite provides a special "Hanc Igitur" if you use Eucharistic Prayer I, The Roman Canon, the oldest canon dating from the 5th century and formerly the only choice. It is during this portion of the prayer that the priest says the words of consecration. Following the words of consecration which end, "Do this in memory of me," the celebrant says:

> **Let us proclaim the mystery of faith.**
> **All: Christ has died,**
> **Christ is risen,**
> **Christ will come again.**

Or, whichever of the four memorial acclamations is used by your church.

The priest then continues the Eucharistic Prayer ending:

> **Through him,**
> **with him,**
> **in him,**
> **in the unity of the Holy Spirit,**
> **all glory and honor is yours,**
> **almighty Father,**
> **for ever and ever.**
> **All: Amen.**

But this is the "Great Amen." You have just said "yes" to the resurrection and you might want to make your "amen" bigger than a simple recited response. Because it is so well-known, many couples have found the "Amen" from the film *Lilies of the Field* an involving, enthusiastic affirmation. There are many other "Amen" arrangements, however, and your choice would be easy to teach during the warm-up session, if you wish everyone to sing, or it may be solo material.

Alternative Canons

The authorized preface-canons are frequently replaced by couples who work with their priest in designing a wedding ceremony more to their own taste. Numerous books and magazines like *Worship* offer a choice of Eucharistic Prayers, some especially composed for a wedding, others centering on a theme of Christian action which may have particular importance to you. Of course, couples have written their own, asked friends to develop one for them, or borrowed one from a ceremony they've admired or their priest has celebrated. Such prayers are generally shorter and written in simpler, more direct and contemporary language that may have greater appeal for you.

If your priest encourages you, experiment with writing a preface-canon, editing a composite of the authorized versions, or discovering your own among the published choices. A California couple composed this Eucharistic Prayer:

> The Lord is with us in this
> Time of joy and sacrament.
> Let us celebrate.
> Let us praise the Lord in celebration
> And show him the gifts we bring.
>
> We have as gift:
> Plain bread and simple wine,
> Tokens of our lives.
> We have as gift:
> The love that brought us together
> From all over,
> To joy in the marriage of friends.
> We have as gift:
> The sacrament we witness,
> The gift which wife and husband
> Have made holy together.
> And we have as gift:
> Christ's perfect gift to his Father,
> and to us,
> The gift of his life
> Lived in constant sacrament.

When he lifted the bread and told his friends, "Take this: eat it; this is my body," and when he lifted his cup and told his friends, "Now drink this; this is my blood; this is the new promise," he promised that whenever we would come

together to make gifts holy he would be with us and bring his
gift and take part with us in our praise.

> Our prayer, therefore is to the Father:
> These are our gifts,
> Gifts of life, of friends
> Of sacred love
> and divine love.

> May your face be pleased and serene
> As you look upon these gifts
> May you take them up as you took up
> The gifts of your servant Abel, a just man,
> The sacrifice of Abraham, our patriarch,
> And that which Melchisedech set before you,
> A holy sacrifice,
> A victim without blemish.

> We ask you, Father, to accept these gifts.
> They are gifts in Christ
> They are blessed by Christ's presence
> They are tokens of Christ.
> Accept them through him.
> Through him
> You make holy
> You make alive
> You make blessed
> and you give to us
> these and all good things.
> Through him
> and with him
> and in him
> is given to you, Father,
> together with the Holy Spirit,
> all honor,
> all glory,
> Forever
> Amen.

And another found a prayer they liked in *Cross Currents:*

Preface:

We give you praise and thanks, Almighty Father,
that you are God,

creator and Father of all men.

You know us and so we live
You love us and so we are your people.

Blessed are you, Father, that you have given us
   this day and this hour.

Blessed are you, Father, in all the things you have made:
   in plants and in animals and in men,
   the wonders of your hand.

Blessed are you, Father, for the food we eat;
   for bread and for wine and for laughter
   in your presence.
Blessed are you, Father, that you have given us
   eyes to see your goodness in the things you have made,
   ears to hear your word,
   hands that we may touch and bless and understand.

We give you thanks that, having made all things, you keep them
   and love them. And so, with all your creation, we praise you,
   through our Lord Jesus Christ, saying:
   Holy, holy, holy
   Lord God of all things
   Heaven and earth are filled with your glory.
   We bless your name,
   Holy is he who reveals your presence among us.

We bless your name.

Canon:

And so we offer you, most merciful Father,
through your Son Jesus Christ,
this sacrifice of praise.

You have chosen us to be your children,
you have called us to a life of joy and love;
you have given us your beloved Son . . . .

We ask for peace everywhere on earth,
peace among all men who still do not know
that we are brothers.
We ask that, loving one another in the bonds of peace,
we may love you as your Son has loved you.

98

Through him we praise you, Father,
through your Son Jesus Christ.
He has revealed your love to us.
He is the image and the incarnation of your presence.
He has become man for us.

Though he is the first-born of all creation,
you sent him from heaven to a virgin's womb.
He took flesh in that womb
and was born of the virgin and of the Holy Spirit.
He did all things that were pleasing to you:
he grew and he obeyed and he loved you
even to his death for us on the cross.

Before he was handed over to undergo the suffering he
accepted for us,
    thereby to free us from death and selfishness and sin
    to bring light to a darkened world,
    to make a new covenant of love and mercy
    he took bread into his hands, gave thanks, broke
    and gave it to his friends, saying:

TAKE THIS AND EAT. THIS IS MY BODY WHICH IS TO
BE BROKEN FOR YOU.

In the same way, he took the cup, gave thanks, blessed and
gave it to his friends, saying:

TAKE THIS AND DRINK.
THIS IS THE CUP OF MY BLOOD,
OF THE NEW AND EVERLASTING COVENANT
FOR THE FORGIVENESS OF SINS
AND THE PROMISE OF LIFE FOREVER.
WHENEVER YOU DO THESE THINGS, YOU WILL
BE COMMEMORATING ME.

And so, Lord God, we commemorate now that he
    suffered and died for us
that he has triumphed over death and lives forever
glorious in his resurrection. . . .

We pray that before the eyes of all men
we may live your Gospel and be witness to Christ's
presence,
that we may support one another in love,

that our hearts may be open to the poor, the sick, the
   unwanted,
to all who are in need.
We pray that thus we may truly be the Church of Jesus
   Christ,
serving one another out of love for you.

And so, Lord God, we eat of this body and drink of this
   blood
of your Son Jesus Christ
as the sign of our faith
and as the food of our life in Christ.

Through him, and with him, and in him,
you are blessed and praised,
Almighty God our Father,
together with the Holy Spirit,
now and forever.
Amen. *

Still a third couple were attracted by this "Table Prayer"
from the book *Prayers, Poems and Songs* by Huub Oosterhuis. The author suggests that, if possible, this be sung
antiphonally by the leader, the choir and all present.

May peace be yours and peace be yours.
May all that is good and makes for happiness
come upon both of you.
May peace be with you all
and in the whole world.

If you, there in your inaccessible light,
you who are God,
if you see us and hear us here,
if we exist for you,
accept then our words of thanksgiving,
this song of great surprise,
on this day which you have made.

We who are simply people
and whose lives are short
have never seen you,
but we venture to sing your name

* "An Experimental Liturgy," by John L'Heureux, from *Cross Currents,* Spring
1967. Copyright © 1966 by John L'Heureux. Used by permission.

and in the words of people
we call you, with the names of centuries
we look for you,
O eternal, living God.

You said, "Let there be light,"
and the light was born;
you saw that it was good,
the land of the morning,
earth and heaven
and all the vaults of water and fire;
you saw that the trees were good
and all the beasts very good
and all the birds perfect;
then you said, "O man,"
and man was born;
but you saw man
and that he was lonely
and could not be comforted,
and so created him man and woman;
you changed and directed all paths
so that these two might find each other —
we thank you, God,
for having done it like this
and in no other way.

I ask you, God, complete them and bless them,
make them become more and more human
and let them experience in their bodies
that they are called
to be as good as God to each other,
that they may become more and more
like him who is your image, your Son,
Jesus of Nazareth, the new man;
he has shown us what life is,
what love does,
becoming man for others
and giving himself, heart and soul,
to this world.

For, on the evening before his suffering and death,
as a sign of the spirit which filled him,
he took bread in his hands and broke it

and gave it to his friends with these words:
take and eat, my body for you.
Do this in memory of me.

He also took the cup with the words:
this is the cup of the new covenant,
my blood, shed for you
for the forgiveness of your sins.
Do this in memory of me.

O God, who are greater than all sin, all death,
and who made the son of men rise again,
you will also never let these two be lost.

Let nothing in them be lost,
because of today.
Keep them alive and let death,
which separates and makes everything dark and empty,
never come upon them.
Let them never tire of each other,
so that they may not falter,
for this world passes,
but love does not pass —
it is like the sea,
flashing like fire and stronger than death.

Keep them together in love,
write their names in the palm of your hand,
write them in your heart,
because of their friends, ourselves,
because of your son, the son of men,
who lives with you
now and for ever.

We ask this, God, and with the words
which Jesus has given us
we come to you and sing "Our Father."

Our Father, who art in heaven,
hallowed be thy name.
Thy kingdom come.
Thy will be done,
on earth, as it is in heaven.
Give us this day our daily bread,
and forgive us our trespasses,

as we forgive those who trespass against us,
and lead us not into temptation,
but deliver us from evil.

Receive this bread
and share it with each other
and drink from this cup;
and know that he will be your God
for ever. *

The Communion Rite

Celebrant: **Let us pray with confidence to the Father in the words our Saviour gave us:**

All: **Our Father. . . .**

There are several vocal arrangements of the "Our Father," but most are quite difficult to learn quickly and well for a congregation that is not used to singing together. However, there is an infectious West Indian melody sung by several of today's popular folk singers which might qualify if you would like this prayer sung rather than recited. Whatever your decision, everyone should participate.

The Nuptial Blessing

Originally couples were married within the wedding traditions of their families and local community. The Church's first role in the ceremony was as guest, invited to lend prestige to the occasion. Eventually, as a courtesy and to add a certain cachet, the custom grew of asking the priest or bishop to give a blessing usually over the marriage bed.

The rite provides three forms of the nuptial blessing and you may choose one of them. Within the choices are options to shorten the prayer, a very good idea. The second selection has become a most popular choice, chiefly because it is a more equal blessing of both husband and wife rather than principally of the wife's service to her husband. The third is concise and has a nice traditional-modern sound.

The priest faces the bride and bridegroom and, with hands joined, says:

* From *Prayers, Poems & Songs,* by Huub Oosterhuis. Copyright © 1970 by Herder and Herder, Inc. Used by permission.

My dear friends, let us turn to the Lord and pray
that he will bless with his grace this woman (or N.)
now married in Christ to this man (or N.)
and that (through the sacrament of the body and blood of
    Christ)
he will unite in love the couple he has joined in this holy
    bond.

*All pray silently for a short while. Then the priest extends
his hands and continues.*

Father, by your power you have made everything out of
    nothing.
In the beginning you created the universe
and made mankind in your own likeness.
You gave man the constant help of woman
so that man and woman should no longer be two, but one
    flesh,
and you teach us that what you have united
may never be divided.

Father, you have made the union of man and wife so holy a
    mystery
that it symbolizes the marriage of Christ and his Church.

Father, by your plan man and woman are united,
and married life has been established
as the one blessing that was not forfeited by original sin
or washed away in the flood.

Look with love upon this woman, your daughter,
now joined to her husband in marriage.
She asks your blessing.
Give her the grace of love and peace.
May she always follow the example of the holy women
whose praises are sung in the scriptures.

May her husband put his trust in her
and recognize that she is his equal
and the heir with him to the life of grace.
May he always honor her and love her
as Christ loves his bride, the Church.

Father, keep them always true to your commandments.
Keep them faithful in marriage

and let them be living examples of Christian life.

Give them the strength which comes from the gospel
so that they may be witnesses of Christ to others.
(Bless them with children
and help them to be good parents.
May they live to see their children's children.)

And, after a happy old age,
grant them fulness of life with the saints
in the kingdom of heaven.

(We ask this) through Christ our Lord.

All: Amen.

If one or both of the parties will not be receiving communion, the words in the introduction to the nuptial blessing, "through the sacrament of the body and blood of Christ," may be omitted.

If desired, in the prayer, "Father, by Your Power," two of the first three paragraphs may be omitted, keeping only the paragraph which corresponds to the reading of the Mass.

In the last paragraph of this prayer, the words in parentheses may be omitted whenever circumstances suggest it.

Choice two

In the following prayer, either the paragraph, "Holy Father, you created mankind," or the paragraph, "Father, to reveal the plan of your love," may be omitted keeping only the paragraph which corresponds to the reading of the Mass.

Let us pray to the Lord for N. and N.
Who come to God's altar at the beginning of their married
    life
so that they may always be united in love for each other
(as now they share in the body and blood of Christ).

All pray silently for a short while. Then the priest extends his hands and continues:

Holy Father, you created mankind in your own image
and made man and woman to be joined as husband and wife
in union of body and heart
and so fulfill their mission in this world.

Father, to reveal the plan of your love,

you made the union of husband and wife
an image of the covenant between you and your people.
In the fulfillment of this sacrament,
the marriage of Christian man and woman
is a sign of the marriage between Christ and the Church.

Father, stretch out your hand, and bless N. and N.

Lord, grant that as they begin to live this sacrament
they may share with each other the gifts of your love
and become one in heart and mind
as witnesses to your presence in their marriage.
Help them to create a home together
(and give them children to be formed by the gospel
and to have a place in your family).

Give your blessings to N., your daughter,
so that she may be a good wife (and mother),
caring for the home,
faithful in love for her husband,
generous and kind.
Give your blessings to N. your son,
so that he may be a faithful husband
(and a good father).

Father, grant that as they come together to your table on
    earth,
so they may one day have the joy of sharing your feast in
    heaven.

(We ask this) through Christ our Lord.

All: Amen.

Choice three

My dear friends, let us ask God
for his continued blessings upon this bridegroom and his
    bride (or N. nd N.)

*All pray silently for a short while. Then the priest extends
his hands and continues:*

Holy Father, creator of the universe,
maker of man and woman in your own likeness,
source of blessing for married life,
we humbly pray to you for this woman

who today is united with her husband in this sacrament of
  marriage.

May your fullest blessing come upon her and her husband
so that they may together rejoice in your gift of married love
(and enrich your Church with their children).

Lord, may they both praise you when they are happy
and turn to you in their sorrows.
May they be glad that you help them in their work
and know that you are with them in their need.

May they pray to you in the community of the Church,
and be your witnesses in the world.
May they reach old age in the company of their friends,
and come at last to the kingdom of heaven.

(We ask this) through Christ our Lord.

All: Amen.

Again, it should be possible for you and your priest to
substitute a prayer or work out an adaption, perhaps bringing
together what you find most significant in each of the
options. Remember, though, that this is the prayer that the
Church prays for you:

> Friends, let us ask God for his continued blessings upon
> this bride, Susan, and this bridegroom, David.

> (all pray silently)

> Father, to reveal the plan of your love, you made the
> union of husband and wife an image of the covenant
> between you and your people.

> Lord, grant that as they begin to live this sacrament
> they may share with each other the gifts of your love
> and become one in heart and mind. Help them to create
> a home together. Give your blessings to Susan so that
> she may be a good wife and mother, faithful in love,
> generous and kind. Give your blessing to David so that
> he may be a good husband and father, faithful in love,
> generous and kind.

> Lord, may they both praise you when they are happy
> and turn to you in their sorrows. May they be glad that
> you help them in their work and know that you are
> with them in their need. May they pray to you in the

107

community of the Church, and be your witnesses in the world. May they reach old age in the company of their friends and come at last to the kingdom of heaven. Through Christ our Lord.

All: Amen.

The Rite of Peace

This is another golden opportunity for the two of you to reinforce and strengthen the sense of community which you have tried to establish among your wedding guests. The peace ceremony has its root in the warm greeting exchanged by early Christians in recognition of their unity with one another. This symbol of communion among guests is a happy prelude to your communion with Christ whose spirit is the source of your fraternity:

Celebrant: **Lord Jesus Christ, you said to your apostles:**
        I leave you peace, my peace I give you.
        Look not on our sins,
           but on the faith of your Church.
        And grant it the peace and unity of your kingdom
        where you live for ever and ever.

    All: **Amen.**

Celebrant: **The peace of the Lord be with you always.**

    All: **And also with you.**

Celebrant: **Let us offer each other the sign of peace.**

Acting as a gracious host and hostess, it is up to you to stimulate response to this invitation. At a wedding, people feel a bit more magnanimous than usual, eager to see you close, offer congratulations, and share their satisfaction with others, so this should be easy. You might first exchange the kiss with each other, then bring it to your celebrant, next to your witnesses and parents. If the group is small the two of you may move together among your families and friends offering a kiss or embrace or handshake and thanking them for being with you. One priest reports with satisfaction that an otherwise staid wedding broke into a mild joyful hysteria at this point as the bride, laughing and crying, hugged her friends. Ideally, his and her relatives and friends will be mingled together, symbolizing the merging of two families.

However, if you must have a "groom's side" and a "bride's side," then the bride might walk along the aisle of his side and he along hers. When the crowd is large, the official witnesses or parents might take the back half of the church.

During the ritual, instrumental music may be played or a song sung: "Shalom," "Let There Be Peace on Earth (Let It Begin with Me)," "They'll Know We Are Christians by Our Love (We Are One in the Spirit)" or one of many others.

Hawaiian couples for whom a flower lei is traditional wedding adornment often use the lei, circle of love, in the peace rite. Traditionally when a lei is placed around a person's neck, that person is kissed, so the bride and groom remove their leis and let them be passed from neck to neck as the kiss of peace is exchanged. Those for whom this ritual seems too frivolous during a Mass, sometimes enjoy it at their reception.

Communion

On the road to Emmaus, the Apostles met Jesus who had died three days before and they did not know him. "And when he had sat down with them at table, he took bread and said the blessing; he broke bread and offered it to them. Then their eyes were opened and they recognized him." (Luke 24:30-31) Hence the unity of Christians is always recognized in the ritual act of breaking the bread and sharing it.

> All: Lamb of God, you take away the sins of the world: have mercy on us.
> Lamb of God, you take away the sins of the world: have mercy on us.
> Lamb of God, you take away the sins of the world: grant us peace.

The celebrant mixes a small bit of bread with the wine and prays quietly. Then:

Celebrant: This is the Lamb of God
who takes away the sins of the world.
Happy are those who are called to his supper.

> All: Lord, I am not worthy to receive you,
> but only say the word and I shall be healed.

The Roman ritual grants the bride and groom the privilege of receiving under both kinds. Depending on the custom in your church, your guests, too, may receive both bread and wine. In very, very few areas, the two of you may even distribute the food and drink to your friends, a beautiful emphasis of your ministerial role in the ceremony and a suggestion of the role of service to others which the two of you will share in your marriage. Whether or not you may actually minister the gifts, it is an appropriate gesture if you stand with the priest and assist him.

This Eucharist is, after all, the union of Christ with his people of which, as the rite constantly tells you, your marriage is a living sign. Perhaps future changes in the ritual will make this truth more evident by visibly underscoring it through establishing the distribution of gifts as a privilege of the married couple. In a ceremony where such a right was granted, we saw a mother receive for the first time in three decades from her son and his new wife.

During the communion processional lively songs celebrating your love for one another and the love of the community for each other should be sung. It is good to select at least one simple, familiar song that all may sing, such as "Kumbaya," "Lord of the Dance," or "Let Us Break Bread Together," but there is generally time, too, for a solo or small group treatment of a favorite of yours. The prayerful silence after communion is a particularly good time for a thoughtful solo like Clarence Rivers' "God Is Love" or "If We Only Have Love," by Jacques Brel.

The rite provides you with a choice among three post-communion prayers:

Choice one

Lord,
in your love
you have given us this eucharist
to unite us with one another and with you.
As you have made N. and N.
one in this sacrament of marriage
(and in the sharing of the one bread and the one cup),
so now make them one in love for each other.

(We ask this) through Christ our Lord.

110

Choice two

Lord,
we who have shared the food of your table
pray for our friends N. and N.,
whom you have joined together in marriage.
Keep them close to you always.
May their love for each other
proclaim to all the world
their faith in you.

(We ask this) through Christ our Lord.

Choice three

Almighty God,
may the sacrifice we have offered
and the eucharist we have shared
strengthen the love of N. and N.,
and give us all your fatherly aid.

(We ask this) through Christ our Lord.

All: Amen.

THE CLOSING RITE

There is one more blessing to be given, then a joyful song and you exit gleefully.

Before the final blessing is a good time for any announcements that will make things easier for your guests. If everyone present is invited to a reception afterward, your lector or best man might say: "The Mass is almost over, but our celebration continues. If anyone can offer a ride or needs a ride to the reception, please see one of the ushers who will make arrangements. Maps are available in the back of the church." Or guests might be directed to the church garden for a receiving line or to the church hall for refreshments. If you or the church wish to discourage rice throwers, say so now, although a notation in your program should be sufficient.

The Final Blessing

In the United States there are four options for this prayer. All are structured so that the priest makes a plea for one aspect of your happiness and your guests respond with an "amen." You may consider this an excellent summation of what has been said during Mass and in the marriage rite or, if

Where you go, I will go, and
where you stay, I will stay.
Your people shall be my people,
and your God my God. Where you
die, I will die, and there I will
be buried. I swear a solemn oath
before the LORD your God: nothing
but death shall divide us.

— Ruth 1

your ceremony has tended to be wordy, you might think this
unnecessarily redundant. Probably you can shorten it.

Choice one

God the eternal Father keep you in love with each other,
so that the peace of Christ may stay with you
and be always in your home.

℞. Amen.

May (your children bless you,)
your friends console you
and all men live in peace with you.

℞. Amen.

May you always bear witness to the love of God in this world
so that the afflicted and the needy
will find in you generous friends,
and welcome you into the joys of heaven.

℞. Amen.

And may almighty God bless you all,
the Father, and the Son, † and the Holy Spirit.

℞. Amen.

May God, the almighty Father,
give you his joy
and bless you (in your children).

℟. Amen.

May the only Son of God have mercy on you
and help you in good times and in bad.

℟. Amen.

May the Holy Spirit of God
always fill your hearts with his love.

℟. Amen.

And may almighty God bless you all,
the Father, and the Son, † and the Holy Spirit.

℟. Amen.

Choice three

May the Lord Jesus, who was a guest at the wedding in Cana,
bless you and your families and friends.

℟. Amen.

May Jesus, who loved his Church to the end,
always fill your hearts with his love.

℟. Amen.

May he grant that, as you believe in his resurrection,
so you may wait for him in joy and hope.

℟. Amen.

And may almighty God bless you all,
the Father, and the Son, † and the Holy Spirit.

℟. Amen.

Choice four

May almighty God, with his word of blessing, unite your
   hearts in the
never-ending bond of pure love.

℟. Amen.

May your children bring you happiness, and may your
   generous love
for them be returned to you, many times over.

℟. Amen.

May the peace of Christ live always in your hearts and
in your home.
May you always have true friends to stand by you, both in joy
and in sorrow.
May you be ready and willing to help and comfort all who come
to you in need.
And may blessings promised to the compassionate be yours in
abundance.

℞. Amen.

May you find happiness and satisfaction in your work.
May daily problems never cause you undue anxiety, nor the
desire for earthly possessions dominate your lives.
But may your hearts' first desire be always the good things
waiting for you in the life of heaven.

℞. Amen.

May the Lord bless you with many happy years together, so
that you may enjoy the rewards of a good life.
And after you have served him loyally in his kingdom on earth,
May he welcome you to his eternal kingdom in heaven.

℞. Amen.

And may Almighty God bless you all,
the Father, and the Son, † and the Holy Spirit.

℞. Amen.

The last blessing, "And may Almighty God bless you all,"
which is meant for everyone present might be invoked by the
two of you as a final testimony to your ministry.

Celebrant: Go in the peace of Christ or **The Mass is ended,
go in peace** or **Go in peace to love and serve
the Lord.**

All: Thanks be to God.

Recessional

As the last words are spoken, the bride and groom join hands
to exit amidst a blast of triumphant, jubilant music. Because
everyone is distracted by looking at you, instrumental music,
a solo or a very well known song works best here. No one
should have to be reading words from his program when he
would rather be watching you walk (skip) down the aisle,

hoping to catch your eye. (Why not stop if you wish?) Look for a good, strong, happy exit sound. Beethoven's purposeful, exhilarating *Ode to Joy* has it; so does this song from *Godspell* whose simple, positive words are part of the sound:

Light of the World

You are the light of the world
You are the light of the world
But if that light's under a bushel
It's lost something kind of crucial
You gotta stay bright to be the light of the world

You are the salt of the earth
You are the salt of the earth
But if that salt has lost its flavor
It ain't got much in its favor
You can't have that fault and be the salt of the earth

So let your light so shine before men
Let your light so shine
O that they might know some kindness again
We all need help to feel fine
(let's have some wine)

You are the city of God
You are the city of God
But if that city's on a hill
It's kind of hard to hide it well
You gotta stay pretty in the city of God

So let your light so shine before men
Let your light so shine
O that they might know some kindness again
We all need help to feel fine
(let's have some wine)

You are the light of the world
You are the light of the world
But the tallest candlestick
Ain't much good without a wick
You gotta live right to be the light of the world.*

116

Have your music continue until everyone is out of the church, following after you in a glad procession. If your attendants are carrying baskets of flowers, they might exit down the aisle distributing these among your friends. Where possible, the music can follow you right into the street, leading your guests to the nearby reception place or playing as you get into waiting cars.

Go, the Mass is ended, but the celebration continues.

BRIEF WORDS ABOUT RECEPTIONS

Everyone loves a party, and that's all a reception is — one good happy party with more going for it than most because it has a glad, shared focus: you.

Your reception is a two-way receiving. Your friends are greeting you as husband and wife and you two are receiving them into your new relationship. Traditionally, the reception begins with a receiving line with the bride's mother at the head followed by her husband if he chooses, then the groom's mother or parents, the bride, groom, and female attendants. A receiving line is a good idea if the wedding is large because it insures that you will at least be able to say "hello" to everyone. Hopefully, it won't have to wait for your arrival at the reception place, especially when this is some distance from the church, but can be formed spontaneously as you exit smiling from your ceremony while you and your guests are at an emotional high. Where the church has a cheerful outdoor area this is a grand setting on a warm, sunny day, but the back of the church is fine. If friends will be at your ceremony who won't be going to the reception (a practice best avoided), it is important that you have a chance to see each other, thereby increasing the imperativeness of having a church receiving line. When the guest list is small, however, and if there won't be a great time-lapse between church ceremony and reception, skip the formality of a receiving line. Make sure, though, that you will get around to welcoming everyone. One bride and groom guaranteed this

118

> . . . Then there was another wedding, many years
> later during the "eighth day of creation," in
> Cana of Galilee. The mother of Jesus was there,
> and Jesus also was invited, together with his
> disciples, to the wedding. Again there was
> rejoicing and again there was a blessing.
> Jesus, anticipating marriage with his own
> bride, renewed married love with a miracle.
> Henceforth there would always be sufficient
> "wine" for the Christian celebration of
> married love. . .   — *Eugene S. Geissler*

thoughtfulness by themselves pouring a round of champagne.

Although there is an understandable tendency to put down the elaborate and expensive reception that leaves the parents or the bride and groom practically in hock, where the wedded couple is only occasionally glimpsed in transit, too busy to enjoy their own party, and at the beck and call of the photographer, the idea of reception deserves no such put down. (Sometimes paying for "the best" is a substitute for thinking.) The desire to feast, to toast, to dance, to sing, to talk with one another is, and always has been, an integral part of weddings, a natural reaction to the joy of what you have done and, depending on the outlook of you and your friends toward liturgical things, at least as important a way of creating community.

In fact, one of the most "spiritual" weddings we ever went to, in the sense that we were made to recognize the deep importance the couple put on the actual act of getting married and the need they felt to share their decision with friends whose support they sought and to whom they offered their support, was almost entirely "reception." Forty guests were invited for the weekend beginning Friday evening with dinner, followed by the ten minute ceremony the next morning, a scrumptious, generous buffet, much wine, and later a swim and an informal gathering for sandwiches at night. The bride and groom departed Sunday morning.

Contributing to the spontaneous fun of this wedding was the couple's attitude toward children. They encouraged guests to bring them and asked a teen-age friend to supervise. She enlisted a pal — necessary because the children were of assorted ages — and planned a special "party" on the edges of the adults' activities. The festivity of the children floated in and out of our consciousness adding to the merriment, but they disappeared magically at all the right moments.

The excellent candid photography of this wedding also made a point. The couple never disappeared; no one was aware of a photographer staging scenes, yet there was a fine collection of visible memories to remind us of an important occasion.

Receptions should be as individual as you two and as unique as the particular and perhaps diverse customs and traditions of your families and culture. Dance the native dances, the tarantella and the hora, let your aunt sing, encourage toasts, share ethnic foods. This pays tribute both to the values of older family members and to the understanding and appreciation of young friends.

Traditions, even unfamiliar ones, almost always enhance a festival. Attend to such ancient ritual acts as cake-cutting, where a shared slice symbolizes a shared life, and bouquet-throwing.

As a souvenir for yourselves set out a guest book in a conspicuous spot and encourage everyone to sign and comment. Albert Einstein, seeking improvised remarks, posted the following "Ordinance" next to his guest book:

> Men, women and little children
> Enter yourself in this little book
> But not with clumsy words
> The way people mumble everywhere,
> Only with verses polite and tender
> As in the august poet's manner.
> Don't worry; simply exert yourself
> And you'll certainly be on the right track!

Or, instead, you might prepare ahead a large piece of parchment and assign a friend to equip himself with the proper materials, collect the marriage certificate after the ceremony, and mount it on the paper, a job quickly done. Provide felt pens and have all the guests sign and comment (briefly), testifying to their witness of your wedding. The

120

friend of a Pennsylvania bride and groom absconded with the signed parchment, illustrated it with gay flowers and symbols, and had it framed as a wedding present. This handsome reminder of their day now hangs in the couple's dining room.

Ideally, the really significant thing about your reception is that as many people as are important to you come and have a good time. And the sophisticated bride and groom know that a good time can be had quite simply. What friends remember and care most about your wedding is that they were *there,* not that it was punch and cake, or chicken rather than roast beef, three courses instead of five, a strolling troubadour in place of an orchestra, domestic champagne rather than imported.

If the church has a reasonably attractive place to offer you for a reception (wondrous transformation can be wrought with imagination), some couples have discovered this a very satisfying arrangement, sustaining the mood as they move swiftly from one celebration to another. Why not have the food brought by friends? Most would be pleased to make this kind of personal contribution to your day. Those who hate to cook can offer decorations or another talent. Ask for this kind of help in lieu of wedding presents. Your guests probably won't pay attention to this, but will appreciate the idea.

Or, how about a real breakfast, the wedding cake, a nut Danish or a pancake stack. Refreshing idea! Or maybe a picnic. A Georgia couple, planning such a reception, were so flexible about their wedding and so enthusiastic about their meadow and their picnic that they issued an invitation with a rain date!

Well, brief words. Of course, there is no right and wrong reception, large, small, indoors, outdoors, catered affair, best silver, paper cups. There is only one essential: that you two are *visible,* creating a very warm committed feeling between your guests and yourselves and among your friends . . . and that you are obviously. . .

Enjoying!

Go to it then, eat your food and enjoy it, and drink your wine with a cheerful heart; for already God has accepted what you have done. *[Ecclesiastes 9:7]*

"MIXED MARRIAGES"
AND MARRIAGES OUTSIDE OF MASS

Not very long ago a couple contracting a "mixed" marriage found the rubrics making extremely stressful what should be one of life's most delightful experiences.   The Church, in an effort to confront the couple with its disapproval and its concern for the faith of the Catholic, insisted that the wedding take place in the Catholic church, seldom permitted the non-Catholic within the altar rails (sometimes relegating the bride and groom to the rectory), and had both parties sign their promise to raise their children as Catholics. It grated. It surely did.

Recently the spirit of ecumenism and a recognition of he couple's most human right to marry have softened the rictions. Officially Pope Paul VI has issued an apostolic determining the norms for a mixed marriage, and the n bishops have responded with their own statement

. . . Two working together are better than one.
They share the reward as the life-bond is spun.
For if they should fall, one will lift up the
other. . . . If two lie together, how warm they will
be! But cold is the night of the man wholly free,
With no one to need him, depend on him, feed him,
With love and communion to follow and lead him
As love moves the two to a chord that is three.
Then joy will reach out in the raddle of love
To fill and resound, return high above. So
love must expand to vibrate in others; The hard,
joyous venture of living together grows richer
threefold with the spirit above; grows vibrant
and strong, a raddle of love.*

—*Nick Hodsdon*

on its implementation. The result is the opportunity for a couple to celebrate their marriage in an open, understanding atmosphere which respects both religious traditions, highlighting much that is common in their outlook toward the bond of marriage and toward children, and avoiding what might offend either individual or their families and make obvious any disunity.

The local bishop has jurisdiction over the mixed marriage, and from him a dispensation is obtained in order that the Catholic may enter into a marriage valid in the eyes of the Church. Generally the approach to the chancery is made through the parish church of the Catholic. When applying for such a dispensation, the Catholic must affirm his intention to do everything possible to remain in the Catholic

---

* From the book *The Raddle of Love: Songs and Ideas for Weddings,* Abingdon Press, 1973. Lyrics © 1970 by Nick Hodsdon. (Based on Ecclesiastes 4:7-12; "raddle" means to interweave, twine together.)

faith and to do all in his power to see that any children are baptized and raised as Catholics. The non-Catholic must be aware of these intentions of the Catholic, but the Church no longer requires that the non-Catholic make any sort of promise or sign anything. In fact, the dispensation does not depend on the non-Catholic's agreement to raise children as Catholics. It is enough to know that the couple are in communication on this subject, aware of the problems it might create and together seeking a viable determination.

The Church has promulgated two rites of marriage to be used by couples entering a mixed marriage. The first, the "Rite for Celebrating Marriage Outside Mass," may be used by two Catholics desiring a ceremony without Mass or by a Catholic marrying a baptized Christian. This rite emphasizes the generally shared Christian belief toward marriage as a sacrament. The second, "Rite for Celebrating Marriage Between a Catholic and an Unbaptized Person," omits any mention of Christ and of sacrament and suggests that the blessing and exchange of rings be omitted if this is not the custom of one of the parties. Both rites are similar to the rite for celebrating marriage within the nuptial Mass, with many of the same options, but they are flexible in permitting omissions or adaptions and substitutions where this would make the ceremony more meaningful and acceptable to the non-Catholic.

In the celebration of these rites the priest is the principal minister, but a non-Catholic clergyman may and should assist in delivering the welcome, readings, prayers, blessings and homily.

Below are the official rites utilized in the marriage ceremony of a Catholic with a non-Catholic when celebrated in a Catholic church or principally by a Catholic priest. The subject should never come up of who actually "marries" you because, of course, you marry yourselves. Exclusive of the parts of the Mass, the elements of these rites are not very different from what is described in the previous chapters, and you will find all options and commentary included in those chapters.

Rite For Celebrating Marriage Outside Mass When Both Parties are Baptized Christians

1. *The Entrance Rite* — The same as described in that

chapter. You may choose an opening prayer from among the options "unless a brief pastoral exhortation seems more desirable." In other words your celebrants should say whatever they and you like.

2. *The Liturgy of the Word* — There may be three Scripture readings chosen from among the options presented in this chapter.

3. *The Homily* — which might emphasize the common Christian concept of marriage.

4. *The Rite of Marriage* — The commentary and options presented in the chapter, "The Exchange of Vows and Rings," apply. The marriage rite will include the priest's request to you to state your marriage intentions, your declaration of consent, the priest's reception of your consent, and the blessing and exchange of rings.

5. *General Intercessions and Nuptial Blessings* — You may choose a nuptial blessing from among the options presented in the chapter "The Liturgy of the Eucharist" and also use the prayer of the faithful, if you desire, in a structure like this:
The first part of the nuptial blessing of your choice, followed by a period of silent prayer or the petitions of the prayer of the faithful with the response of your guests in a prayer of your and their creation, concluded by the remaining portion of the nuptial blessing you have chosen.

6. *Conclusion of the Celebration* — The rite concludes with the Lord's Prayer and a blessing. This can be simply "May Almighty God bless you all, the Father, and the Son, † and the Holy Spirit" or you may choose a longer blessing from among the four optional blessings for the end of Mass as presented in the chapter, "The Closing Rite."

Rite for Celebrating Marriage Between a Catholic and an Unbaptized Person

1. *The Entrance Rite* — As above. Even omitted, if you wish.

2. *The Liturgy of the Word* — The three Scripture readings

125

from among the options or only one if this seems more suitable.

3. *The Homily* — Which would probably not speak of sacrament or "Christian" marriage. Marriage, of course, is not a Christian invention.

4. *The Rite of Marriage* — As described in this chapter with variations the couple find appropriate. The invitation to state your intentions differs from the other rites in omitting mention of Christ and sacrament. The official rite suggests the following, but your celebrant, of course, may substitute his own words or those you choose:

My dear friends, you have come together in this
church so that the Lord may seal and strengthen
your love in the presence of the Church's minister
and this community. In this way you will be strength-
ened to keep mutual and lasting faith with each
other and to carry out the other duties of marriage.
And so, in the presence of the Church, I ask you to
state your intentions.

The couple then give their consent to one another and it is received by the priest, followed by the blessing and exchange of rings if this is desired.

5. *General Intercessions and Nuptial Blessings* — These may be used if the couple wish or they may be omitted if circumstances require. If used, the first part of whichever nuptial blessing the couple chooses from among the options in the "Liturgy of the Eucharist" chapter is given, then a period of silent prayer or the petitions of the prayer of the faithful, concluded by this blessing as presented in the rite:

Holy Father, creator of the universe,
maker of man and woman in your own likeness,
source of blessing for married life,
we humbly pray to you for this woman
who today is united with her husband in the bond of
 Marriage.

May your fullest blessing come upon her and her husband
so that they may together rejoice in your gift of married love.

May they be noted for their good lives,
(and be parents filled with virtue).

Lord, may they both praise you when they are happy
and turn to you in their sorrows.
May they be glad that you help them in their work,
and know that you are with them in their need.
May they reach old age in the company of their friends,
and come at last to the kingdom of heaven.

(We ask this) through Christ our Lord.

R. Amen.

6. *Conclusion of the Celebration* — You may use the
Lord's Prayer or, if the nuptial blessing has been
omitted, another prayer by the priest. This might be
followed by the simple "May Almighty God bless
you. . . ,"although a reference to the triune God may
not be suitable, or a formula from among the options
for the blessing at the end of Mass as presented in the
chapter, "The Closing Rite."

As you can see the rites are very simple, wide open,
depending upon your celebrants and your improvisation.

Marriage with a non-Catholic can, of course, be performed within the nuptial Mass. Only the two of you can
decide if this would be comfortable for both of you and your
families. As intercommunion is permitted in only a few
places (and a dispensation sometimes takes awhile to get —
plan ahead), it might underline the differences between you
if the non-Catholic is not participating in the Eucharist. On
the other hand, one groom handled this situation very
gracefully, illustrating his respect and understanding. During
communion, which he did not receive, he sang the Jefferson
Airplane's song:

Today

Today, I feel like pleasing you more than before
Today, I know what I want to do but I don't know what for
To be living for you is all I want to do
To be loving you, it'll all be there when my dreams
   come true.

Today, you'll make me say that I somehow have changed

Today, you look into my eyes I'm just not the same
To be any more than all I am would be a lie
I, so full of love I could burst apart and start to cry.

Today, everything you want, I swear it all will come true.
Today, I realize how much, I'm in love with you
With you standing here, I can tell the world what it
    means to love.
To go on from here, I can't use words 'cause they don't
    say enough.

Please, please, listen to me, it's taken so long to come true
But it's all for you.*

The Church also recognizes that there are circumstances
where a Catholic rite celebrated in a Catholic church by a
priest precludes a marriage ceremony where the greatest
harmony between a bride and groom and their families can
be achieved, and might, in fact, lead to lasting estrangement.
It is now easily possible to obtain a dispensation so that the
Catholic can be married in a non-Catholic church or
synagogue, according to the rite of that church and where the
non-Catholic clergyman is the principal celebrant. In this
case, a priest may assist, his presence reassuring to the
Catholic's family and testifying to the desire of the Church to
recognize and bless this marriage.

Currently the directive from the National Conference of
Catholic Bishops and from most non-Catholic churches to
their congregations is that there be a certain "integrity of the
liturgy." This means that whichever church or synagogue is
the scene of the marriage has the primary responsibility for
its celebration using its rite; its minister invites the consent,
receives the vows and gives the principal nuptial blessing. The
rule is that the rites of the two faiths must not be celebrated
alternately. At the present time, too, most chanceries require
that the marriage be celebrated in a "sacred place," i.e., in a
church or synagogue. Only exceptional circumstances are
officially allowed a "suitable secular setting."

The churches of almost all denominations are aware,
however, of the changing needs of the marriage rite in a
pluralistic society, and rites everywhere are being revised with

128

a pastoral eye to options and freedom. In addition there is continuous dialogue among the churches and still more ecumenical liturgies might be expected in the future. It is good for a couple planning a mixed marriage to have available to them the rites of both their churches. Although your ceremony may be primarily one rite or the other, you will be delighted to discover the similarities in structure and thought that do exist among most marriage rites, and you might borrow certain content and tradition from each.

Even when you are limited by your choice or your church to the strict utilization of either a Catholic or a non-Catholic rite, there is plenty of opportunity for words and song, gesture and decoration, to acknowledge the two religions and the uniqueness of your particular marriage. And, of course, you will discover individual priests, ministers and rabbis joyfully ahead of the rubrics, many celebrating with the tacit consent of bishops who find it difficult to legislate broad liberal policy but do understand diversity.

In a mixed marriage it is more important than ever that you shop around for your celebrants, finding cleric friends (or friends of friends) who will work with you in developing a ceremony in which you and your families are at home. It is very difficult for some parents to see a son or daughter married in a ceremony strange to them. The presence of a clergyman of their own faith and familiar hymns and prayers and symbols will make them feel like welcome participants rather than awkward onlookers. The choice of a church is important, too. One church lends itself more graciously to a mixed marriage ceremony than another. It is perfectly possible to find a simple community church that will welcome his college chaplain and her parents' minister to celebrate the ceremony, all done with you properly dispensed and registered. Be persistent and keep looking.

And certainly for some couples entering a mixed marriage and for their families, the ceremony will be much more relaxed and enjoyable for all if it takes place in the "neutral territory" of a home or garden. You'll surely be able to find celebrants who'll understand and accommodate this.

When you have decided on the "feel" you wish your celebration to have, introduce the two clergymen who will celebrate so they will have an opportunity to plan together. If only one of you has a cleric friend and family pressure doesn't dictate another choice, ask your friend to suggest a colleague of the other religion who will be receptive to your ideas and have intriguing thoughts of his own.

In a recent ceremony between a Catholic and Protestant, celebrated within a Nuptial Mass and in a parish church where the couple were allowed no tampering with the liturgy, the minister acted as lector, introducing each of the parts of the Mass. He and the priest, together, greeted the couple and welcomed the guests. The minister read the selections for the Liturgy of the Word, delivered the homily and shared in giving the nuptial blessing. "Amazing Grace," a Protestant hymn and a favorite of the groom's mother, was played among the more contemporary music choices of the couple. Both fathers brought up the offertory gifts and gave them to their children.

In a much more free-spirited ecumenical ceremony, a Jewish-Catholic couple were married in a Catholic church under a magnificent flower canopy, traditional setting for the Jewish ceremony. The music included the singing of *Fiddler on the Roof's* "Sunrise, Sunset":

> ". . . under the canopy I see them, side by side.
> Place the gold ring around her finger,
> share the sweet wine and break the glass. . . " *

Wine was shared and bread broken in a non-sacramental expression, a Jewish and even pagan rite of hospitality, community and thanksgiving long pre-dating the act of Christ. The glasses were broken. The Scripture reading was taken from the Old Testament and there were several readings from secular literature. The welcome and blessings were delivered by both rabbi and priest. A friend of the couple had made the celebrants matching wedding vestments in distinctive styles marked with symbols appropriate to each religion. The banners, program and invitation saluted both faiths.

The breaking of the bread and drinking of the wine were

---

* Lyrics of "Sunrise, Sunset," by Sheldon Harnick, from the production *Fiddler on the Roof,* copyright © 1964 by Sunbeam Music Inc. (A Metromedia Co.) 1700 Broadway, New York, N.Y. 10019. Used by permission only. All rights reserved.

130

explained in a commentary by the priest in such a way that Catholic, Protestant and Jewish guests present felt comfortable sharing this meal with the bride and groom.

The success of the ceremony was confirmed at the reception when the father of the Catholic groom arose to give his toast:

"L'Chaim," he began. And ended:

"Shalom."

APPENDIX

Our life is frittered away by detail.
—Thoreau

This last section of the book contains more suggestions for songs, readings, decorations, etc., you may want to use in your wedding. Some of the songs in particular have established themselves as enduring favorites; others were popular when this book was being written and should be replaced by songs popular now when you're marrying yourselves. The same goes for the readings. Be contemporary by all means.

Books and Magazines

Bride's Magazine and *Modern Bride* are filled with ideas for color schemes, traditional and zany dress, and lists and lists of what you *must* do and *absolutely* need. Fun to see how much you can eliminate.

Then there are the standard references: *Amy Vanderbilt's New Complete Book of Etiquette,* 1970 (Doubleday, also Bantam Books); *Emily Post's Etiquette,* 12th edition, 1969 (Funk & Wagnalls, also Pocket Books); *McCall's Engagement and Wedding Guide,* 1972 (Saturday Review Press).

Warning: Get your head on right before opening. As tools to help you separate your essential from your forget-it, they're useful. But remember it's your wedding, and you're like no one else. Use the information, don't let it use you.

Invitations, Mass Booklets, Banners

Some of the stuff offered in catalogues is junk, much of it sentimental. But there are many colorful, workable basics that you can build from. Send for the catalogues and decide.

For the most joyous and contemporary indoor, outdoor, say-it-warmly invitation ideas: Conception Abbey Press, Conception, Missouri 64433.

132

For bright, simple invitation covers: Leaflet Missal Guild, 1999 Shepard Road, St. Paul, Minn. 55116.

For invitation covers and a handy-sized folder for your ceremony program: Sacred Design, 840 Colorado Avenue South, Minneapolis, Minn. 55416.

If it's posters and banners you're looking for, write to The Liturgical Press, Collegeville, Minn. 56321. We especially like their collection of Robert Fox's Full Circle posters interpreted by Judith Savard. Carol Spain and Kathi are represented too.

Another good source, especially for banners: Abbey Press, St. Meinrad, Ind. 47577.

Today is the first day of the rest of our lives

I live on Earth at present
and I don't know what I am.
I know that I am not a category
I am not a thing — a noun.
I seem to be a verb,
an evolutionary process —
an integral function of the universe.

     —*R. Buckminster Fuller**

for all that has been
THANKS
for all that will be
YES
    —*Full Circle*

We need to have people
who mean something to us.
People to whom we can turn
knowing that being with them
is coming home.

    —*Bernard Cooke*

Be of love a little more careful
than of everything.

    —*e. e. cummings*

Love is a harsh and terrible thing
to ask of us, but it is the only answer.

    —*Dorothy Day*

---

* From *I Seem to Be a Verb,* Bantam Books. This is a hodgepodge of revealing quotes. Read it through, turn it over and read it through again, then turn it sideways and read it, then. . .

open your heart capture the joy of TODAY *—Abbey Press*

Love is union under the condition of preserving one's integrity. *—Erich Fromm*

For it is only framed in space that beauty blooms.

—Anne Morrow Lindbergh

Love should be essentially an act of the will. . .It is a decision, it is a judgement, it is a promise. *—Erich Fromm*

I wonder what the world is doing today?

—Henry David Thoreau

Choose life!

Some day after we have mastered the winds, the waves, the tides, and gravity, we will harness for God the energies of love, and then for the second time in the history of the world man will have discovered fire. *—Teilhard de Chardin*

No man truly has joy unless he is living in love.

—St. Thomas Aquinas

Acclaim the LORD, all men on earth,
worship the LORD in gladness;
enter his presence with songs of
exultation.

—Psalm 100 (NEB)

We belong to each other; our oneness is a part of us, and by joining in this ceremony, you have made it a part of your lives, too. *—Anonymous*

May the outward and inward man be as one. *—Socrates*

As for conforming outwardly, and living your own life inwardly, I do not think much of that.

—Henry David Thoreau

The question is always whether we will act—whether we will teach the children and heal the sick, help the weak and venerate the old. *—Robert Kennedy*

where
charity and love are
there is God.

—St. John

The true vocation of man is to find his way to himself.

—Hermann Hesse

134

God made the world for this moment, and we are on the brink of heaven knows what discoveries.

—Katherine Mansfield

... this is my prayer, that your love may grow ever richer and richer in knowledge and insight of every kind, and may thus bring you the gift of true discrimination.

—Philippians 1:9

You belong to the universe. The significance of you will forever remain obscure to you, but you may assume that you are fulfilling your significance if you apply yourself to converting all your experiences to highest advantage of others. You and all men are here for the sake of other men.

—R. Buckminster Fuller

Waterside Wedding

Once there was a couple who lived near the water. They met on the water, loved on the water and loved the water, and so they were married on the banks of the Maryland shore: she in a long, white lace dress bought in an end-of-season clearance sale in a shop that was not for brides, and he in white pants and a bright blue shirt; their feet were bare, and so were those of most of their guests, even his mother, and especially her father who thought that this was the way weddings should be. Here are some of the things they did:

Their invitation (Abbey Press) issued in the names of both families announced their theme with a water scene and a quote from Hesse:

> dear friend we are sea and land
> It is not our purpose to become each
> other—it is to recognize each other—
> to learn to see the other and honor
> him for what he is—each the other's
> opposite and complement.

The reception was going to be a clam and lobster bake. First it had to be prepared. Some helped for a while, and others stood around watching. And then there was music which called people together for the celebration, a Grateful Dead song from the album *Workingman's Dead* which spoke of Uncle John's Band "playing to the tide. . ."

And of course there were banners:

> O God, your sea is great
> and my boat is so small.
>
> Man at his best, like water,
> serves as he goes along.
>
> —*Laotzu*

> We are all islands in a common sea.
> —*Anne Morrow Lindbergh*

The priest explained a little why the couple chose to be married by the water, symbol of rebirth and refreshment, borrowing in part from Rachel Carson's *The Edge of the Sea*:

> The shore is an ancient world, for as long as there has been an earth and sea there has been this place of the meeting of land and water. Yet it is a world that keeps alive the sense of continuing creation and of the relentless drive for life. Each time that I enter it, I gain some new awareness of its beauty and its deeper meanings, sensing that intricate fabric of life by which one creature is linked with another, and each with its surroundings.*

His rap, too, played to the water motif seeking the couple's response to Jesus' invitation to "come with me, and I will make you fishers of men."

During the offertory the food which had been brought as gifts by the guests was blessed, and the bride and bridegroom, who had stayed with their respective parents until this moment, left their parents' sides, were sent forth by them, and came together to marry themselves in front of their families and friends and the priest.

The bridegroom recited a poem by William Butler Yeats that symbolized for him a certain hope that he had for their life together:

---

*Copyright © 1955 by the Houghton Mifflin Company. Used by permission.

136

The White Birds

I would that we were, my beloved,
    white birds on the foam of the sea!
We tire of the flame of the meteor,
    before it can fade and flee;
And the flame of the blue star of twilight,
    hung low on the rim of the sky,
Has awaked in our hearts, my beloved,
    a sadness that may not die.

A weariness comes from those dreamers,
    dew-dabbled, the lily and rose;
Ah, dream not of them, my beloved,
    the flame of the meteor that goes,
Or the flame of the blue star that lingers
    hung low in the fall of the dew:
For I would we were changed to white birds
    on the wandering foam: I and you!

I am haunted by numberless islands,
    and many a Danaan shore,
Where Time would surely forget us,
    and Sorrow come near us no more;
Soon far from the rose and the lily
    and fret of the flames would we be,
Were we only white birds, my beloved,
    buoyed out on the foam of the sea! *

Immediately following their exchange of solemn, joyous
promises, there was the consecration, the solemn, joyous
promise of Christ.

Because the bride and groom were leaving for two years
of service in Africa, at the final blessing their best man spoke
for all present:

For Friends Only

Easy at first, the long of friendship
Is, as we soon discover
Very difficult to speak well, a tongue
With no cognates, no resemblances
To the galimatias of nursery and bedroom
Court rhyme or shepherd's prose

And unless often spoken soon goes rusty
Distance and duties divide us,
But absence will not seem an evil
If it makes our re-meeting
A real occasion. Come when you can:
Your room will be ready.*

A Short Collection of Readings

Most love poetry is not suitable for your wedding. It speaks of love found on a summer's day and lost in the winter. It is bitter, biting, bothered by ego and distraction. Or it is shallow, mushy, rhyming heart and depart, hand and garland. Readings from Sartre, Baldwin, Simone de Beauvoir, and Shakespeare have worked well at weddings, I am told, and if you are into them you know where to find what you want.

Californians (and others) read Kenneth Patchen, ecologists read Black Elk and Ehrlich and Nader and Dubos and Lynn White Jr., and every third bride and groom reads from Gibran's *The Prophet* (although Rilke and Hesse and Anne Morrow Lindbergh express better reverence for time and space in human relationships). Some who wept at *Love Story* borrow Jenny's and what's-his-name's vows: Elizabeth Barrett Browning's "When our two souls stand up erect and strong ... " this portion of Walt Whitman's "Song of the Open Road":

> . . .I give you my hand!
> I give you my love, more precious than money,
> I give you myself before preaching or law;
> Will you give me yourself? Will you come
>   travel with me?
> Shall we stick by each other as long as we live?

One couple wove the saying of an old valentine sent by her father to her mother into their comments, and another incorporated the family's traditional Thanksgiving Day prayer into their celebration.

The best readings, probably, are those composed by the bride and groom or someone who knows them well.

Better still, maybe no readings at all: a Mass and marriage rite honed to the bare essentials, with music and environment and gestures telling the story.

But if you want readings other than, or in addition to, the usual Scripture readings — or are looking for life-style ideas to direct your own decisions and perhaps inspire your composition about them — there are a few books that have proven fruitful for couples in recent years. These include *There Is a Season* by Eugene S. Geissler (Ave Maria Press), *Celebration of Awareness* by Ivan Illich (Doubleday), *The Intimate Marriage* by Howard and Charlotte Clinebell (Harper and Row), *Listen to Love* by Louis Savary (Regina Press), *Gift from the Sea* by Anne Morrow Lindbergh (Pantheon), *Open Marriage* by Neva O'Neill and George O'Neill (M. Evans & Co.), *Meditations* by Dorothy Day (Newman), *The Freedom of Sexual Love* by Joseph and Lois Bird (Doubleday), *They Call Us Dead Men* by Daniel Berrigan (Macmillan), *Sacred Bridge: Liturgical Parallels in Synagogue and Early Church* by Eric Werner (Schocken), *Love and Will* by Rollo May (Norton), *The Art of Loving* by Erich Fromm (Harper and Row), *e. e. cummings Poems 1923-1954* (Harcourt Brace Jovanovich), *The Covenant of Peace: A Liberation Prayer Book* compiled by Brown and York (Morehouse-Barlow), *A Time for Love and the New Sexuality* by Eugene C. Kennedy (Doubleday), anything by R. Buckminster Fuller, and even *The Last Whole Earth Catalog.*

For specific readings, consider the following:

> If I truly love one person I love all persons,
> I love the world, I love life.
> If I can say to somebody else, "I love you,"
> I must be able to say, "I love in you everybody,
> I love through you the world, I love in you also myself."
>
> —*Erich Fromm*

Because God's love is in me it can come to you from a
different and special direction that would be closed if
He did not live in me, and because His love is in you it
can come to me from a quarter from which it would not
otherwise come. And because it is in both of us, God has
greater glory. His love is expressed in two more ways in which
it would not otherwise be expressed: that is, in two more
joys that could not exist without Him.*

—*Thomas Merton*

Men Marry What They Need, I Marry You

Men marry what they need. I marry you,
morning by morning, day by day, night by night,
and every marriage makes this marriage new.

In the broken name of heaven, in the light
that shatters granite, by the spitting shore,
in air that leaps and wobbles like a kite,

I marry you from time and a great door
is shut and stays shut against wind, sea, stone,
sunburst, and heavenfall. And home once more

inside our walls of skin and struts of bone,
man-woman, woman-man, and each the other,
I marry you by all dark and all dawn

and learn to let time spend. Why should I bother
the flies about me? Let them buzz and do.
Men marry their queen, their daughter, or their
        mother

by names they prove, but that thin buzz whines
        through:
when reason falls to reasons, cause is true.
Men marry what they need. I marry you.**

* From *Seeds of Contemplation* by Thomas Merton. Copyright © 1949 Our Lady
of Gethsemani Monastery. Reprinted by permission of New Directions Publishing
Corporation.

**From *I Marry You,* by John Ciardi, © 1958 by Rutgers, the State University.
Reprinted by permission of the author, who adds: "I'd be willing to permit
reproduction on any wedding program for private use and distribution at no fee as a
souvenir of the wedding. Anyone who likes the poem is certainly entitled to it as a
wedding present. That's part of why it was written."

A Eucharistic Prayer

It is utterly, purely, absolutely right,
O God, our source, our future,
Spirit present in our lives,
that we should give you thanks and praise
at every moment and in every place,
through Jesus Christ, our Lord and brother;
"love one another" was his commandment, his message, his life,
so, as we join to celebrate a new covenant of love,
we pledge ourselves to put all things in our lives together
under the direction and the rule of love.
Grateful for so clear a word, so luminous a sign,
we lift our hearts in praise and sing:

Holy, holy, holy. . .
Blessed be your name, O God,
for you have brightened the pages of our history,
from our father Abraham even until now,
with light of faith and restless striving.
Blessed be your name,
that name by which established gods are overthrown,
established ways are challenged, established tyrannies are
      made to yield to freedom.
Blessed be your name,
the name that sparks the energies of man
to master nature's forces and to build community.
Blessed be your name,
the call to unity and peace and love
which has today concrete expression in N. and N.
Blessed be your name,
a name that we dare speak with Jesus,
who is here among us as our brother,
amazing grace of reconciling and forgiving love.
Through him your Spirit breathes in every place
stirring us out of isolation, into solidarity.
We call upon you now to make that breath of Spirit into
      mighty wind,
to make us one with all our sisters and our brothers,
as N. and N. are one,
as this bread is one, this cup is one.
For Jesus, Lord and brother of us all,

bequeathed to us this sign of charity.
While he was at supper with his friends,
he took bread, gave you thanks and praise, and broke it,
giving it to those he loved and saying to them:
This bread is my body, broken to make you whole.
Take it and share it — all of you.
He took a cup, filled with wine, and gave you thanks and praise.
He gave it to his friends and said:
This cup is my blood, my life, my spirit,
poured out as you must pour out your own selves.
This is forgiveness. Take it and drink it — all of you —
    in memory of me.

We do this, then, our Father, in memory of him
who came to bring the good news to the poor,
to proclaim liberty to captives and to the blind new sight,
to set the downtrodden free;
who took upon himself the death we all must face,
was raised to live again and lend us hope,
gave glory to our fragile flesh and a kingdom model for community.
Let us proclaim the mystery of faith:

Pour out your Spirit on these gifts †
and on ourselves — the Spirit of love and solidarity —
so that N. and N. can offer themselves to one another,
so that all of us can offer our sacrifice, our bodies and our blood,
in union with the fellow-seekers everywhere,
with all the churches, all communities of faith,
with the humble signs of brotherhood we have
    in Paul our pope and N. our bishop,
with all who look to you our God in hope.
Sinners all, but free at last, we trust your mercy
for a place in holy fellowship with all the dead and all your saints.
Everything reflects your glory,
awaits the newness of Christ's kingdom
and the touch and shaping of our living faith.
Through him, with him, in him,
fused into one by the flame of your Spirit,
we sing honor and glory to you, Almighty Father,
    for ever and ever.*

---

* By Robert W. Hovda, from *Liturgy*, May 1972, the journal of The Liturgical
Conference. Copyright © 1972 by The Liturgical Conference. Used by permission.

Do Me That Love

Do me that love
As a tree, tree
Where birds and wind
Sing though they know
How real night is
And no one can
Go on for long
In any way
Do me that love

Do me that love
As the rain, rain
That has voices
In it, the greats'
and fools', poor dead
From old weathers —
Lives considered
And rejected
As ours will be.
The rain comes down
And flowers grow
On the graves of
Our enemies
Do me that love.*

The heavens tell out the glory of God,
    the vault of heaven reveals his handiwork.
One day speaks to another,
night with night shares its knowledge,
        and this without speech or language
        or sound or any voice.
    Their music goes out through all the earth,
        their words reach to the end of the world.
In them a tent is fixed for the sun,
who comes out like a bridegroom from his wedding canopy,
rejoicing like a strong man to run his race.
    His rising is at one end of the heavens,
        his circuit touches their farthest ends;
        and nothing is hidden from his heat.

The law of the LORD is perfect and revives the soul.
 The LORD's instruction never fails,
  and makes the simple wise.
The precepts of the LORD are right and rejoice the heart.
 The commandment of the LORD shines clear
  and gives light to the eyes.
The fear of the LORD is pure and abides for ever.
The LORD's decrees are true and righteous every one,
more to be desired than gold, pure gold in plenty,
 sweeter than syrup or honey from the comb.
 It is these that give thy servant warning,
 and he who keeps them wins a great reward.

 Who is aware of his unwitting sins?
 Cleanse me of any secret fault.
Hold back thy servant also from sins of self-will,
 lest they get the better of me.
 Then I shall be blameless
and innocent of any great transgression.
May all that I say and think be acceptable to thee,
 O LORD, my rock and my redeemer! —*Psalm 19 (NEB)*

 Lord, make me an instrument of your peace!
 Where there is hatred, let me sow love;
 Where there is injury, pardon;
 Where there is doubt, faith;
 Where there is despair, hope;
 Where there is darkness, light;
 Where there is sadness, joy.
 O divine master,
 Grant that I may not so much seek to be
  consoled as to console,
 To be understood as to understand,
 To be loved as to love.
 For it is in giving that we receive,
 It is in pardoning that we are pardoned,
 And it is in dying
  that we are born to eternal life. —*St. Francis of Assisi*

 Come! Let us raise a joyful song to the LORD,
 a shout of triumph to the Rock of our salvation.
 Let us come into his presence with thanksgiving,
 and sing him psalms of triumph.

For the LORD is a great God,
a great king over all gods;
the farthest places of the earth are in his hands,
    and the folds of the hills are his;
the sea is his, he made it;
the dry land fashioned by his hands is his.
Come! Let us throw ourselves at his feet in homage,
let us kneel before the LORD who made us;
    for he is our God,
we are his people, we are the flock he shepherds.
You shall know his power today
    if you will listen to his voice.* —Psalm 95 (NEB)

Growing

Who are you? Who am I? Haunted
By the dead, by the dead and the past and the
Falling inertia of unreal, dead
Men and things. Haunted by the threat
Of the impersonal, that which
Never will admit the person,
The closed world of things. Who are
You? Coming up out of the
Mineral earth, one pale leaf
Unlike any other unfolding,
And then another, strange, new,
Utterly different, nothing
I ever expected, growing
Up out of my warm heart's blood.
All new, all strange, all different.
Your own leaf pattern, your own
Flower and fruit, but fed from
One root, the root of our fused flesh.
I and thou, from the one to
The dual, from the dual
To the other, the wonderful,
Unending, unfathomable
Process of becoming each
Our selves for each other.**

---

* This makes an excellent entrance reading. Perhaps you can set it to music.

**From *Collected Shorter Poems,* by Kenneth Rexroth. Copyright © 1956 by New Directions Publishing Corporation. Reprinted by permission of New Directions Publishing Corporation.

Selecting the Right Music

"People said what they liked best about our wedding was the music," reported one couple. The same probably holds true for many weddings, and so choosing the music for your wedding is no little thing.

The trend now seems to be toward contemporary music, but traditional songs and hymns still work well.

Once you select the songs you want, the next problem is to find the music. Your local music store is usually happy to locate the publisher and order sheet music for you. You can also write directly to the publisher, if you know who it is.

As for religious music, Concordia Publishing House (3558 South Jefferson Avenue, St. Louis, Mo. 63118) has collections of traditional wedding music for the organ, choir, solo, and duet, including Bach's "Jesu, Joy of Man's Desiring" and "The Lord Bless You," Buxtehude's "Lord, Who at Cana's Wedding Feast" and Brahms' "O Jesus, Joy of Loving Hearts."

If you like the Gelineau Responsorial Psalms, you can order them through the Gregorian Institute of America (2115 West 63rd Street, Chicago, Ill. 60636).

For the songs listed below marked WLSM, write to World Library of Sacred Music (5040 North Ravenswood, Chicago, Ill. 60640).

F.E.L. Publications, Ltd. (1543 West Olympic Boulevard, Los Angeles, Calif. 90015) has a wide selection of "folk" religious songs with simple guitar arrangements. They suggest for weddings Ray Repp's "This Is the Day" and "If You're Gonna Love," John Fischer's "Love," Daryl Ducote's "Without Clouds" and Gary Ault's "You Are Loved."

We're especially attracted to *Locusts and Wild Honey,* a collection of songs (both on record and sheet music) by the monks at Weston Priory (Weston, Vermont 05161). Inquire about their planned new album and song book with the same kind of accessible, prayerful and personal sound and a song especially for weddings.

There are a number of excellent songs in *The Sesame Street Songbook* by Jeffrey Moss and Joe Raposo, published by Simon & Schuster, Inc. (630 Fifth Avenue, New York, N. Y. 10020). Also look at *The New York Times Great Songs of the 60's.*

Finally, here's a warning: all these songs are protected under international copyright laws. You are free to sing them at your wedding, but if you decide to go into the publishing business yourself by mimeographing, xeroxing or otherwise reproducing the music or the lyrics for your wedding guests, you are violating the law and you could be sued. If you ask their permission, many publishers will let you run off 100-200 copies of a song without charge—so long as you also print their copyright notice. See the sheet music for the name and address of the person or company that controls the rights.

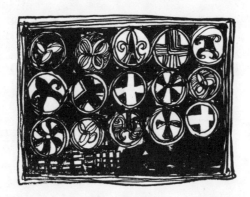

Music for Before the Service
"The Song Is Love"
(also good at offertory or between readings) Mary Travers et al.

"People" Bob Merrill and Jule Styne

"Alfie" Hal David and Burt Bacharach

"Turn! Turn! Turn!" Pete Seeger

"He's Got the Whole World in His Hands"
(He's got Gail and Bill in his hands)

"Somebody Come and Play" Sesame Street

"Friends" Elton John and Bernie Taupin

"We've Only Just Begun" sung by The Carpenters
(maybe in response to vows)

"Today" ("while the blossoms still cling to the vine . . . ")
Randy Sparks

"Look of Love" Hal David and Burt Bacharach

The Goodness of God
Cries Out

Weston Priory
Gregory Norbet, O.S.B.

Lively

To - day the good-ness of God cries_

out, and the wa - ters come to life with your

1.2.3.   VERSES:

sav - ing grace.___ 1. O   Fa-ther of   all   you
2.   Ra- di- ant   is   your
3. To - day you ap - pear   O

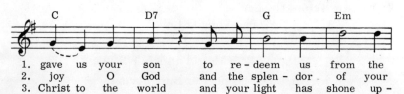

1. gave   us   your   son   to   re - deem   us   from   the
2. joy   O   God   and   the   splen - dor   of   your
3. Christ   to   the   world   and   your   light   has   shone   up -

1. dark - ness_ of   sin.___   To - grace._____
2. love   is a - live,_ a - live.___   To -
3. on_____   us,__ O   Lord.__   To -

* By Gregory Norbet, O.S.B., from the album *Locusts and Wild Honey*, produced by Weston Priory Productions, Weston, Vermont. Used by permission.

Kaleidoscope

Come with me what wonders we'll find,
The ducks on the mill pond that swim in the mind.
Come with me together we'll go,
Where buttercups shoot through the roof of the snow
And many the sight that we'll see,
I'll look in your eyes and see me.

Chorus
K I Kaleidoscope
Love is another color from hope.
Pain is a sep'rate color from joy
How many colors there are to enjoy.

Come with me through valleys of green,
We'll live like the mudlark, deep down in a dream.
Come with me take hold of my hand,
I'll walk you past panthers asleep in the sand
How lucky some people will be,
To look in our eyes and see we.

Chorus
Come with me stay close by my side,
The road is so rocky, the world is so wide.
Come with me and we will go far,
Far is forever where ever we are
How wise is our world and how new
You'll look in my eyes and see you.
*Chorus**

149

Songs for Coming In

"This Is Your Day" Paul Evans—Fred Tobias

"Enter, Rejoice and Come In"

"New World Coming" Barry Mann and Cynthia Weil

"What the World Needs Now" Hal David and Burt Bacharach
(or as response to vows, or as an exit)

"Bridal March" C. Hubert Parry

"Just a Closer Walk with Thee"

"Father, We Gather Here to Praise You" Joseph Roff

"It Is Good to Give Thanks to the Lord" R. F. Twynham

"Never Find Another You" The Seekers

"Shout from the Highest Mountain" Ray Repp (F.E.L.)

Or try some kind of skipping music, or handclapping music, or one long trumpet blast. Perhaps you could be led in by dancers, or your attendants could form a human chain and bring you up.

At the Liturgy of the Word

As a substitute for an Old Testament reading, try the following. The composer, William Flanders, said about this song, "I've always loved girls who are free spirits, and a number of years ago I married one." For this arrangement and others of Flanders' songs write to him at 3714 Harrison Street, N.W., Washington, D.C. 20015.

Rebekah's Song

There's a lonely country town
Where the women all come down
To the well at the end of the day.
When a stranger passes by,
He can't help but wonder why
Ev'ry maid sets down her pitcher
In his way.

Chorus

Will you come to the well fair Rebekah?
Will you leave all your childhood behind?

So begins the serenade
Of a simple village maid

With a spirit independent and bold.
Who, for no apparent gain,
Watered one whole camel train,
'Cause the man who asked
Was tired out and old.
Chorus
But the stranger was a man
From the house of Abraham,
On a quest to which he pledged his very life.
With his camel caravan
He came 'cross the desert sand.
For young Isaac he must try
To find a wife.
Chorus
"Lovely maiden, are you free
To leave home and follow me?
Over miles and miles of desert we will ride.
There in Canaan, where your name,
Will have everlasting fame,
To the son of Abraham
You'll be bride."
Chorus
There's a lonely, country town
Where the women all come down
To the well, at the end of the day.
When a stranger passes by
He can't help but wonder why
Ev'ry maid sets down her pitcher
In his way.*

If during the Liturgy of the Word you would like the Gospel put to music, there are a number of musical versions of the Beatitudes. Try the one in *Locusts and Wild Honey.*

In Response to the Vows
"If We Only Have Love" Jacques Brel
"Bridge Over Troubled Water" Paul Simon
"Special" Sesame Street (as a salute to the groom)

---

* Copyright © 1968 by William Flanders. Used by permission.

"The First Time Ever I Saw Your Face" Ewan MacColl
(salute to the groom)

"Black Is the Color" (salute to the groom,
if it applies to your true love's hair)

"And I Love Her" John Lennon and Paul McCartney
(as a salute to the bride)

"Here There and Everywhere"
John Lennon and Paul McCartney
(salute to the bride)

"They Long To Be Close to You" (salute to the bride)

"If I Were a Carpenter" Tim Hardin
(salute to the bride)

"For Baby (For Bobby)" H. J. Deutschendorf, Jr.
(as a salute to the bride, a soft, gentle love song)

"Turn Around, Look at Me" Jerry Capehart

"If I Ever Needed Someone" Van Morrison

"We're Together" sung by the Hillside Singers

Love Is Here

Weston Priory
Gregory Norbet, O.S.B.

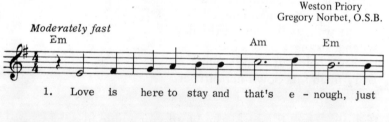

1. Love is here to stay and that's e - nough, just

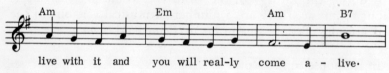

live with it and you will real-ly come a - live·

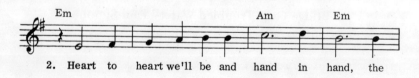

2. Heart to heart we'll be and hand in hand, the

152

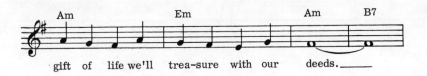

gift of life we'll trea-sure with our deeds. _____

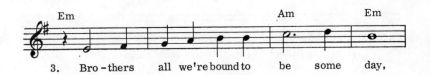

3. Bro-thers all we're bound to be some day,

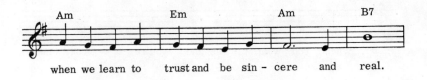

when we learn to trust and be sin - cere and real.

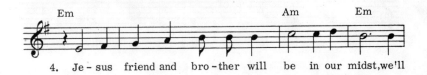

4. Je - sus friend and bro-ther will be in our midst, we'll

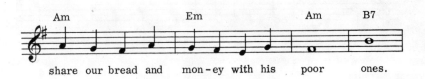

share our bread and mon-ey with his poor ones.

5. Love will be for us our way of life, it's

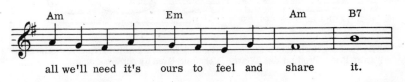

all we'll need it's ours to feel and share it.

153

6. Once a-gain we'll be a - live, a - live,

joy un-end-ing real-ly un-der-stand-ing life.

7. When you want to sing and you're a - lone, just

think of what it is to be a - live, a -

live, for love is here to stay and that's e -

nough, just live with it and you will real-ly

come,___ come a - live.___

* By Gregory Norbet, O.S.B., from the album *Locusts and Wild Honey*, produced by Weston Priory Productions, Weston, Vermont. Used by permission.

154

Follow Me

It's by far the hardest thing I've ever done
To be so in love with you and so alone
Refrain:
Follow me where I go what I do and who I know
Make it part of you to be part of me
Follow me up and down all the way and all around
Take my hand and I will follow too

It's long been on my mind
    you know it's been a long long time
I'll try to find the way that I can make you understand
The way I feel about you and just how much I need you
To be there where I can talk to you when
    there's no one else around
Refrain:
You see I'd like to share my life with you
And show you things I've seen
Places where I'm going to — places where I've been
To have you there beside me and never be alone
And all the time that you're with me
    then we will be at home

Follow me where I go what I do and who I know
Make it part of you to be part of me
Follow me up and down all the way
Take my hand and say you'll follow me
Take my hand and say you'll follow me.*

"Standing at the Threshold" Arlo Guthrie

"The Wedding Song" Buffy Sainte-Marie

"Since You've Asked" Judy Collins

"Now Thank We All Our God" Johann Crueger (1647)

"What Are You Doing the Rest of Your Life?"
from the United Artists' film *The Happy Ending*

"To Be Young, Gifted and Black" Nina Simone

"Song for the Asking" Simon and Garfunkel

"Where Do I Begin?" from *Love Story*

"You've Got a Friend" Carole King

"Bless, O Lord, These Rings" solo or duet with
organ (Gregorian Institute)

"For All We Know" sung by The Carpenters

"One Hand, One Heart" from *West Side Story,*
(a duet for bride and groom if they can sing)

"Love Is" Rod McKuen

"Once I Loved"

Once I loved the wind as it blew
Down from the mountains, over the land.
Once I loved the touch of the sun
As much as I loved the touch of the hand.
And once I loved the smell of the sea,
The feel of the waves rolling over me.
Air and sky, sea and sand,
Once I loved, once I loved.

Once I loved the rain as it fell
Down the window and over the land.
Once I loved the face of the clouds
Almost as much as the touch of a hand.
And once I loved the smell of a rose,
The deep at the bottom of the garden grows.
Fields of flowers, tall and proud,
Once I loved, once I loved.

Once I loved all of God's things
That grew on the earth and over the land.
Once I loved the warmth of a fire,
But never as much as the touch of your hand.
Now I love the feel of your arms
Over, around, all about me.
Once I loved, once I loved,
But never till now.*

156

At the Kiss of Peace

"I'd Like To Teach the World To Sing"

"Let There Be Peace on Earth"

"Peace Will Come" Melanie

"Peace Train" Cat Stevens

During the Offertory

"Everything Is Beautiful" Ray Stevens

"Of My Hands" Ray Repp (F.E.L.)

"Beautiful People" Melanie, a good solo

"Take Our Bread" Joe Wise (WLSM)

"Let Us Break Bread Together" Robert Blue (F.E.L.)

"Within You, Without You" George Harrison

"Stand!" Sly and the Family Stone

"Born Free" John Barry and Don Black

"Bein' Green" Sesame Street,
(an easy one to teach before the service)

"All Good Gifts" from *Godspell*

"Heart of Gold" Neil Young

"I Wish I Knew How It Would Feel To Be Free"
Billy Taylor and Dick Dallas

At Communion

"Lord of the Dance" Sydney Carter,
from *New Hymns for a New Day* (World Council of Churches)

"He is Love" Clair St. Clair and Don Goldie

"We Thank You Father" from *Locusts and Wild Honey*

"How Often Do We Say 'Thank God'"
Kay Anderson and Kathy Holt

"Put a Little Love in Your Heart" Jackie De Shannon

"A Simple Song"
Stephen Schwartz and Leonard Bernstein (from *Mass*)

"We Beseech Thee, Hear Us" from *Godspell*

"Valley to Pray" Arlo Guthrie

"In Christ There Is No East or West"

157

"Glory to God" Clarence Rivers (WLSM)
"God Is Love" Clarence Rivers (WLSM)
"Kum Ba Yah"
"All Kinds of People" Hal David and Burt Bacharach
"Day by Day" from *Godspell*
"Sons of God" James Thiem (F.E.L.)
"May the Lord Bless You" Ken Meltz (WLSM)
"Where Charity and Love Are" Joseph Roff

Music for Exiting
"Put Your Hand in the Hand" Gene MacLellan
"They'll Know We Are Christians by Our Love" (F.E.L.)
"Ode to Joy" Beethoven
"Let's Get Together" Chet Powers
"Aquarius" from *Hair*
"Joy that Knows No End" from *Locusts and Wild Honey*
"The Impossible Dream" from *Man of La Mancha*
"Climb Ev'ry Mountain" from *The Sound of Music*
"Light of the World" from *Godspell*
"With Hearts Full of Joy"

A Record of Our Wedding Choices

	Selection	Page
Opening Prayer	_____	_____
Old Testament Reading	_____	_____
Responsorial Psalm	_____	_____
New Testament Reading	_____	_____
Alleluia	_____	_____
Gospel	_____	_____
Vows	_____	_____
Blessing of Rings	_____	_____
Prayer of the Faithful	_____	_____
Prayer Over the Gifts	_____	_____
Preface	_____	_____
Eucharistic Prayer	_____	_____
Nuptial Blessing	_____	_____
Prayer After Communion	_____	_____
Blessing at the End of Mass	_____	_____

Other Readings   Place in Ceremony

_____   _____

_____   _____

_____   _____

_____   _____

_____   _____

_____   _____

_____   _____

_____   _____

_____   _____

_____   _____

_____   _____

_____   _____

Music Selections

Entrance _____

After Vows _____

Offertory _____

Communion _____

Recessional _____

Other _____

Below are the vows, prayers, and other things we wrote ourselves, as well as our invitations, banners, and the actions we planned for the ceremony:

_____

_____

_____

_____

_____

_____